Suzanne Torres
Joanna Heijmer

Starlight

5

Student Book

OXFORD
UNIVERSITY PRESS

Vocabulary and Language Focus

1 Look, listen and say the names. 01

The Starlight School

Please keep your school neat.

Mr. Alistair McMaster
Principal

Mr. Bob Tidy
School Groundskeeper

We are Class 5A

Miss Shanice London
Teacher

Alex Bean

Lily Bean

Anna Bean

Betty Greenstreet

William Victory

2 Listen and complete the table. 02

Sign up for a penfriend

Full name	Birthday	Address	Brothers/Sisters	Hobbies	Pets
Alex Bean		Bean Cottage, 10 Little Street, Aceton	Lily, Anna	soccer	**(1)** Dog (Bongo)
Lily Bean	September 22		Anna, Alex	**(2)** _____	Dog (Bongo)
Anna Bean			Lily, Alex	**(3)** _____	Dog (Bongo)
(4) _____	**(5)** _____	7 Little Street, Aceton	**(6)** _____	**(7)** _____	**(8)** _____
(9) _____	March 17	**(10)** _____	none	**(11)** _____	**(12)** _____

3 Choose a character from Activity 2. Play *Guess Who* with a partner. 💬

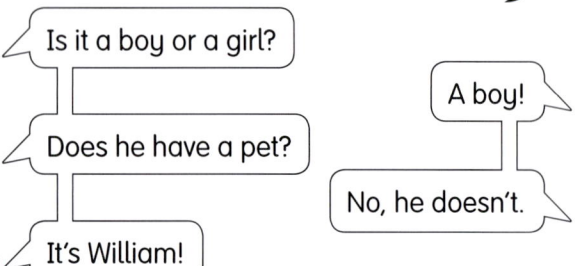

Is it a boy or a girl?

A boy!

Does he have a pet?

No, he doesn't.

It's William!

4 Make questions with the table headings. Ask and answer in pairs. 📝 💬

What …?   When …?   How many …?
Do you …?   Do you have … ?   Where …?

When's your birthday?

It's on August 17!

5 Match the words with the places (1–12). Listen, check and say. 03

auditorium   bike shed   cafeteria   coatroom   drama theater   music hall
principal's office   reception   restrooms   science lab   staff room   tennis court

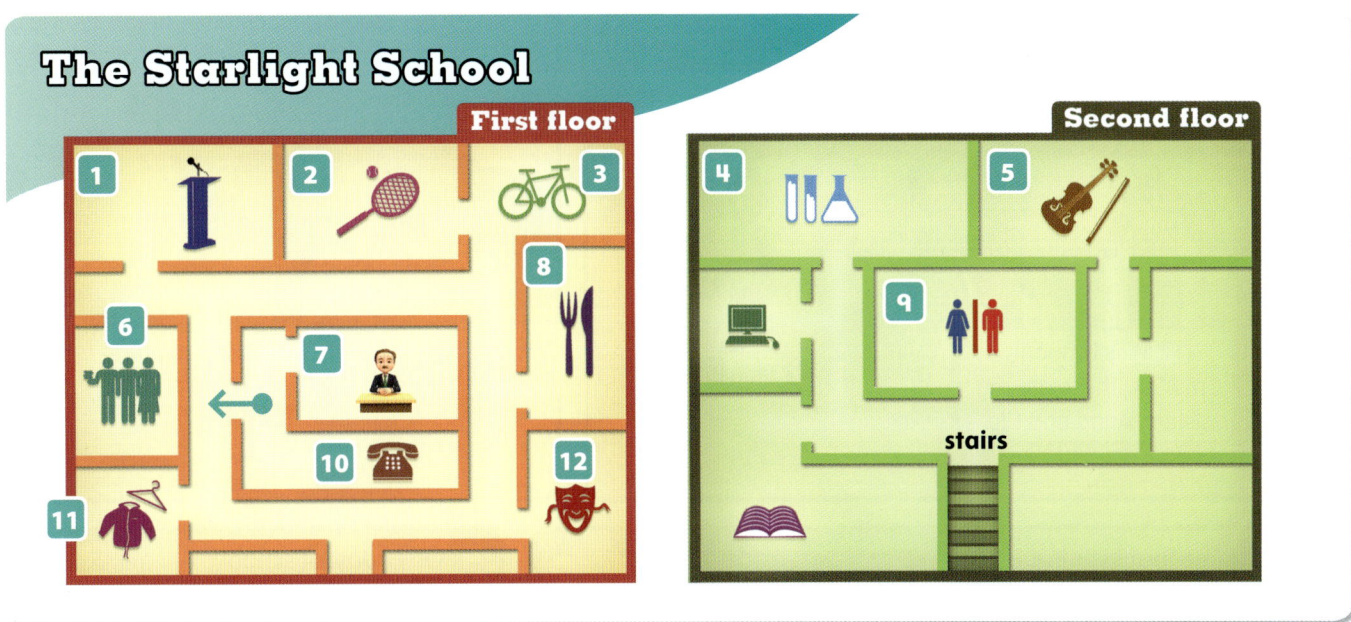

6 Read the notices and write the place.

a
School assemblies
Years 1, 2, 3 – Monday 9:15 am
Years 4, 5, 6 – Friday 9:15 am

b
apple juice $1.25
orange jelly $1.75
ham sandwich $2.99

c
Please wash your hands.

d
Please ask at reception for balls and rackets.

e
DO NOT TOUCH THE PIANO!

f
Please knock and wait if you want to talk to a teacher.

g
Ssh! Drama production in progress!

h
Always wear a bike helmet!

i
Please do not disturb.
(Mr. McMaster is on the phone.)

j
Danger! Chemicals!
Please keep this closet closed!

k
If the receptionist is not here, please ring this bell. ➡
Thanks!

l
Please hang all coats and bags.

7 Look at Activity 5. Listen and say. 04

8 Play *Route Plan* in pairs.

You are in the reception. Turn left. Then turn right. Go straight ahead. At the end of the hall turn left.

3

Summer Break

1 Listen and read the story. 05

2 Act out the story.

Welcome back to school 5A! I'm your new teacher, Miss London.

Hi William!

Hi Miss London! I'm Alex. These are my sisters, Anna and Lily.

Hey Betty!

This week, prepare a presentation about your summer break. Please bring something from your vacation to show us.

I have my plane ticket to France!

I can bring my map of Fun World!

3 At home that evening.

We're worried about our homework, Mom. We didn't go on vacation this year.

Well, you didn't go on vacation, but you did lots of fun activities.

The other students went to interesting places.

But we don't have any tickets or maps to take to school.

Aha! Listen, kids …

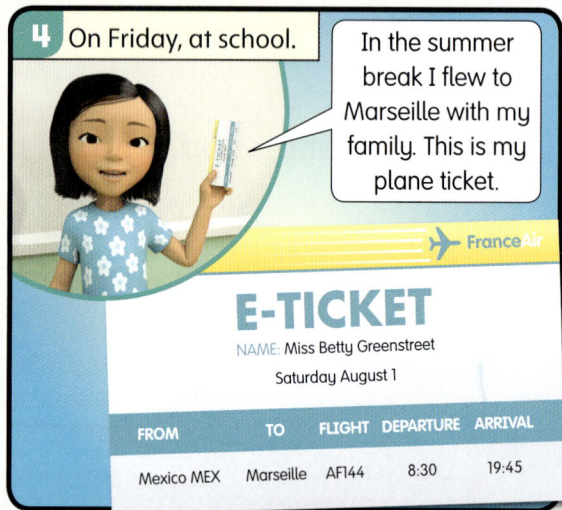

4 On Friday, at school.

In the summer break I flew to Marseille with my family. This is my plane ticket.

France Air

E-TICKET

NAME: Miss Betty Greenstreet

Saturday August 1

FROM	TO	FLIGHT	DEPARTURE	ARRIVAL
Mexico MEX	Marseille	AF144	8:30	19:45

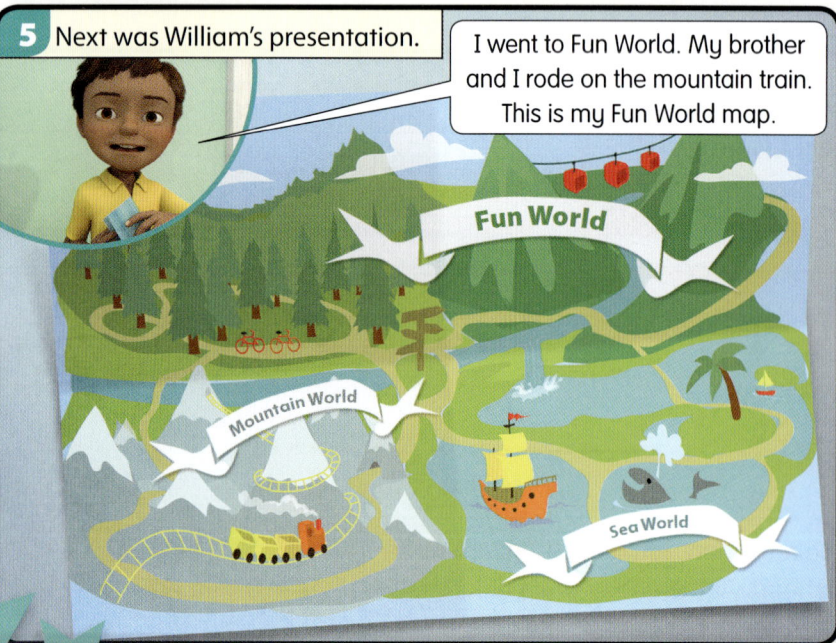

5 Next was William's presentation.

I went to Fun World. My brother and I rode on the mountain train. This is my Fun World map.

Fun World

Mountain World

Sea World

6 Then it was Anna, Lily and Alex's turn.

In the summer, Alex, Lily and I had an adventure. I wrote about it in my diary: Monday August 3. Tonight we camped in a tent. We were all alone! In the night we heard a wild animal.

All alone? Wow! That's scary!

7

TUESDAY, AUGUST 4

Today we explored the countryside. In the morning we went climbing. When we were hungry, we found food.

WEDNESDAY, AUGUST 5

This afternoon we swam in dangerous waters. Then we sailed a ship.

8

9

10

11

12

Vocabulary and Reading

1 Match the words with the pictures (1–12). Listen, check and say. 06

> ant   beetle   centipede   fly   grasshopper   ladybug
> mosquito   moth   snail   spider   wasp   worm

2 Look at Text A. Listen and say the bug. 07

3 Read Text B and answer. 1 min

- What are nocturnal bugs?
- What do you need to study them?

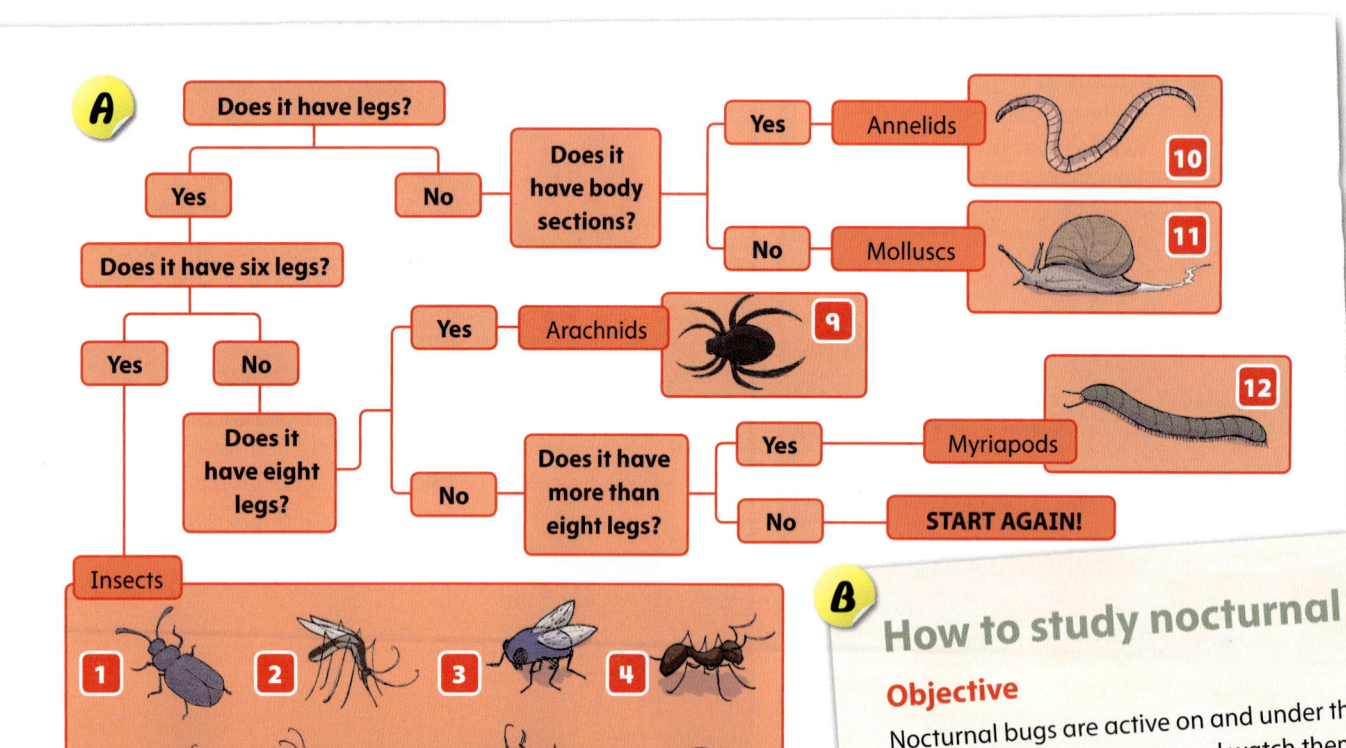

A

Does it have legs?

Yes — No

Does it have six legs?

Does it have body sections?

Yes — Annelids

No — Molluscs

Yes — No

Yes — Arachnids

Does it have eight legs?

No

Does it have more than eight legs?

Yes — Myriapods

No — START AGAIN!

Insects

1   2   3   4

5   6   7   8

10   11   12   9

B How to study nocturnal bugs

Objective

Nocturnal bugs are active on and under the ground at night. Catch these bugs and watch them. Don't forget to free them after the experiment!

Equipment

- a trowel
- a plastic cup
- food (cheese, fruit or meat)
- 4 stones
- a magnifying glass
- a square piece of wood

4 Play *Likes and Dislikes* in pairs.

> Which bugs do you like?

> I like worms, but I don't like ants.

c

The Bugs Poem

The bugs had a meeting by an old chestnut tree.
"Why don't humans like us?" said an angry, young bee.
"Well," said the beetle, "everyone knows
Sometimes moths eat people's clothes."

"Excuse me!" said the moth. "Some beetles eat wood.
They eat doors and furniture! That isn't good!"
"People don't like my legs," said the spider. "They're hairy.
I don't know why, but humans think that we're scary."

"Flies annoy people," said the spider. "Here's how …
They make a lot of noise! They're making noise now!
Spiders are quiet. I'm not telling lies. And
We help humans, because we catch flies!"

"Poor Fly!" said the centipede. "Oh no! Don't cry!
We're all food for animals. It isn't just Fly.
Birds and bats, fish and frogs eat me and you.
We're an important part of the food chain. It's true."

"And I know," said the bee, "sometimes we sting.
It's for our protection. It's a natural thing.
But bees are working in hives as we speak.
They're making honey for humans to eat."

"Hey," said the worm, "I'm ugly and thin,
But when I move through the soil, air and water get in.
I'm useful. I want those big humans to know
That I help all their plants and their flowers to grow."

"Let's tell the world!" shouted the ants.
"We're important to animals, humans and plants!"
"Yes!' said the snail. The grasshopper agreed.
So they all wrote this poem for people to read.

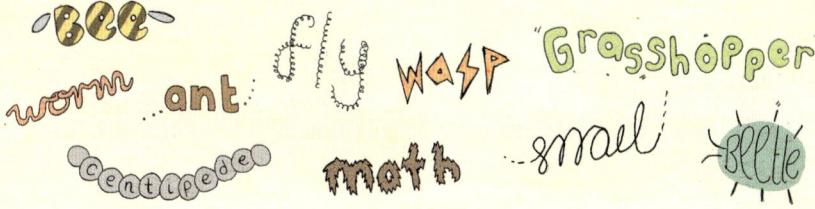  

6 Answer in pairs. Use the phrases in the box.

1 Why don't some people like beetles?

2 Why does Fly cry?

3 Which bugs think they are useful? Why?

4 Do people know bugs are important?

> Because he / she / it / they …
> I (don't) think they …

> Why don't some people like beetles?

> Because they eat doors and furniture!

1 Look at page 7. Read and listen to the poem again. Match the sentence halves. 🎧 08

1 Flies
2 The flies are
3 Bugs
4 Bees
5 The bees are

a sting people.
b make a lot of noise.
c making a lot of noise now.
d working in hives as we speak.
e are important to animals, humans and plants.

2 Complete the chart.

doesn't catch   don't sting   eat   eating   ~~eats~~   jumping   making   working

Simple present				Present continuous (*be* + verb + *–ing*)			
Affirmative	He / She / It	**(1)** _____eats_____	honey.	**Affirmative**	He / She / It	's	**(5)** _____ in the hive.
	They / People	**(2)** _____			Beetles	are	**(6)** _____ wood.
Negative	He / She / It	**(3)** _____	flies.	**Negative**	He / She / It	isn't	**(7)** _____.
	They / Worms	**(4)** _____	people.		They	aren't	**(8)** _____ webs.

3 Listen and number. 🎧 09

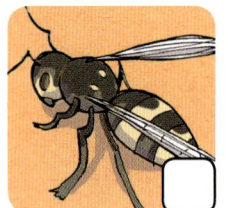     

4 Match the words with the pictures of the bugs. Describe the pictures in pairs. 💬

catch flies   eat plants   eat wood   fly   jump

make holes in the soil   make honey   make webs   sting people   work in a hive

It doesn't sting people. It isn't catching flies now. It's making a web.

It's a spider!

1 **Read part 1 and complete. Read Text B on page 6 again and check.**

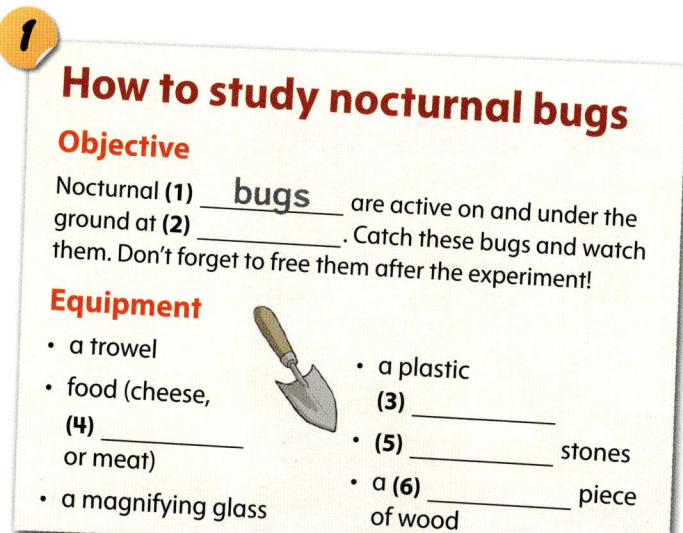

1

How to study nocturnal bugs

Objective

Nocturnal **(1)** __bugs__ are active on and under the ground at **(2)** _____. Catch these bugs and watch them. Don't forget to free them after the experiment!

Equipment

- a trowel
- food (cheese, **(4)** _____ or meat)
- a magnifying glass
- a plastic **(3)** _____
- **(5)** _____ stones
- a **(6)** _____ piece of wood

2

Instructions

1 Cut the cheese, fruit or meat into small pieces. Put the pieces of food into a bag and take them outside.

2 Dig a hole in the ground and put the cup in it.

3 Put the pieces of food in the cup.

4 Leave the cup outside for a night while you sleep.

5 In the morning, study the bugs you find in the cup. Then set them free in the garden again.

Note: Don't go outside at night alone. Ask an adult to help you with the experiment. Ask him or her to come outside if it's dark.

2 **Read part 2 and order the pictures (1–7).**

a [1]   b [ ]   c [ ]   d [ ]

e [ ]   f [ ]   g [ ]

3 **Find the phrases in part 2 and match.**

1 take them outside

e pieces of food

2 put the cup in it

_____

3 set them free in the garden

_____

4 Ask him or her to come outside

_____

a a female adult
b the bugs
c the hole
d a male adult
e pieces of food

4 **Rewrite the sentences using *it* or *them*.**

1 Study the bugs you find. Set the bugs free in the garden.

Study the bugs you find. Set them free in the garden.

2 Get some cheese. Cut the cheese into small pieces.

_____

3 Look at the beetles. Draw and color the beetles.

_____

4 I like bugs. I often read about bugs.

_____

1 Look and say what the lesson is about. 💬

2 Listen and repeat. 🎧 10

1 bird feeder
2 scarecrow
3 greenhouse
4 petal
5 wheelbarrow
6 raspberry
7 pollen
8 watering can
9 stem
10 seeds
11 weeds
12 roots

3 Listen and number the words. 🎧 11

1	greenhouse	☐ raspberry	☐ seeds
☐	pollen	☐ roots	☐ watering can

4 Look and complete the mind map.

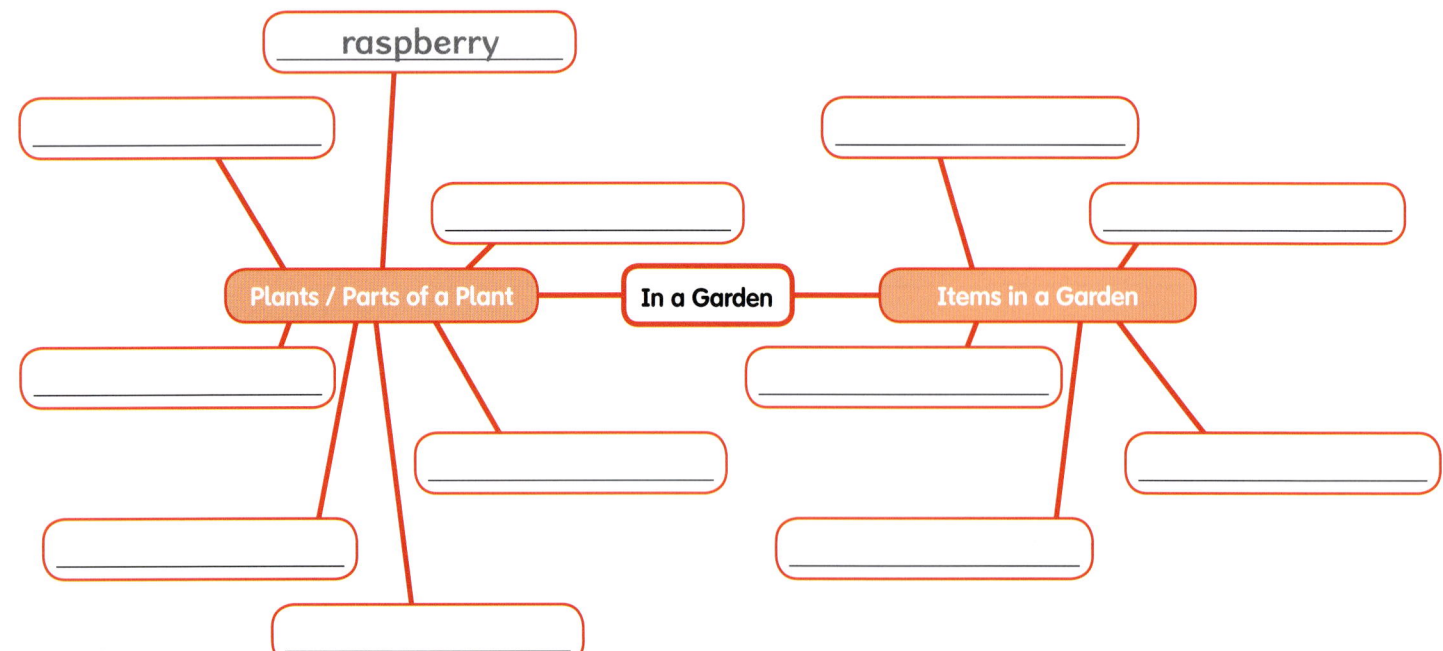

raspberry

Plants / Parts of a Plant

In a Garden

Items in a Garden

Lily's Tune

5 Listen and mark (✔) the fruit and vegetables you hear. 🎵 **12**

- ☐ apples
- ☐ oranges
- ☐ potatoes
- ☐ pumpkins
- ☐ raspberries
- ☐ sweet corn
- ✔ tomatoes

6 Listen again and complete the lyrics.

> A scarecrow scares the birds away.   Here's my greenhouse. It's quite hot.
> I dig the soil and take out weeds.   Sweet corn's growing tall outside.

In my garden, I plant some seeds.
(1) __I dig the soil and take out weeds.__
Bees bring pollen. Then, you know,
Roots and stalks and petals grow,

In my garden, plants and flowers grow.
Roots and stalks and petals grow, you know.

These can help my garden grow:
A watering can, a wheelbarrow.
(2) _____
They come to eat nuts every day.

Here's my trowel, my basket and my hoe.
It's fun to push my wheelbarrow, you know.

(3) _____
Tomatoes are growing in small pots.
This is where the pumpkins hide.
(4) _____

Raspberries are growing in the sun.
Welcome to my garden everyone.

7 Read the lyrics and complete the sentences.

1 I plant some __seeds__ .

2 _____ bring pollen.

3 A _____ and a _____ help the garden grow.

4 A _____ scares the birds away.

5 _____ come to eat nuts.

6 _____ are growing in the greenhouse.

7 _____ are growing in the sun.

8 Play *Guess What* in pairs. 💬

Can you eat it?

No, you can't.

Is it part of a plant?

1 Match the plant names with the pictures and answer in pairs. What do you know about these plants?

1 coconut **2** dandelion **3** mistletoe **4** pea **5** poppy **6** sycamore

2 Listen, read and check your ideas. 🎧 **13**

How Seeds Move

When plants make seeds, the seeds can't all grow close to the plant because they need space. They need to move to a different place. This is called seed dispersal and it happens in different ways.

The wind moves the seeds of some plants. Dandelion seeds are very light. If it's windy, the seeds blow far away from the plant. Poppy seed heads have little holes around the top. When the wind blows, the heads move and the seeds fall in different directions. Sycamore seeds have special wings. They can fly in the wind.

Fruits contain seeds. The fruits of some plants can float on water. Coconut trees grow near water. If a coconut falls into the sea, it travels a long way. If the coconut finds land, a new tree grows.

Some plants, like peas, grow their fruit inside pods. When the fruit is ready, the pods explode and the seeds fly in different directions.

Animals move seeds, too. Some plants have fruit that animals like to eat. If a bird eats an apple, the apple seeds move to a new place in the bird's droppings. Some plants, like mistletoe, have sticky seeds. If an animal passes these plants, the seeds stick to its fur. Then the animal carries the seeds to a new place.

3 Look at the chart and underline more examples of the *Zero Conditional* in the text.

Zero Conditional			
Condition		**Result**	
If	the wind blows	,	the heads move.

4 Read the text again and match the sentence halves.

1 If a plant makes seeds,
2 If seeds grow away from a plant,
3 If the seeds of a plant are light,
4 If the wind blows a poppy seed head,
5 If the peas are ready,

a the pod opens.
b they can blow a long way easily.
c the seeds fall out of the holes.
d the seeds need to move to a different place.
e they have more space.

5 Finish the sentences in pairs.

If seeds have wings, …   If a bird eats fruit, …   If a coconut lands on a beach, …

1 Look and label the pictures. Listen and match the people with the chores they do. 🎧 14

> hang the clothes   pick blackberries   pick pears   put a plant pot in the greenhouse
> put birdseed in the birdfeeder   ~~sweep up the leaves~~

sweep up
the leaves
_____   _____   _____   _____   _____

| 2 | Tim | | Fiona | | Natalie |

 2 Listen again and complete the conversations.

1 Can you sweep up the leaves, please Tim?

   a Yes, of course!

   b (I don't think I can, Mom.)

   c I'm sorry, Mom, I can't.

2 Please can you hang the clothes on the clothesline, then?

   a I don't think I can, Mom.

   b No problem!

   c Yes, of course!

3 Can you put that plant pot in the greenhouse, please, Natalie?

   a No problem!

   b I'm sorry, Mom, I can't.

   c Oh no!

3 Look, listen and repeat. 🎧 15

Perfect Pronunciation

clothesline   greenhouse   blackbirds   blackberries   fish pond

plant pot   birdseed   birdfeeder   pear tree

4 Complete the pairwork cards. Ask and answer in pairs. 📖 119

Can you help me shovel the snow, please?

Sorry, I can't. I have a cold.

1 Look at the pictures.
Why do you think honeybees are important?
Discuss in pairs.

Anna Knows about ...

Honeybees

2 Listen and read along. Number the words in the pictures. 🎧 16

1 honeycomb   **2** nectar   **3** pollen   **4** queen bee   **5** worker bee

Honeybees are important insects and our lives would be very different without them.

Honeybees live in a beehive. There is one queen bee. She is the biggest bee, and she lays all the eggs. She lays about 2,000 eggs every day. A queen bee lives for about five years.

In the beehive, there are about 50,000 worker bees. Worker bees only live for about 40 days. Worker bees do many different jobs. They keep the beehive clean and build the honeycomb. Worker bees fly from the beehive and collect nectar. Nectar is a sweet and sticky liquid in flowers. The nectar is the bees' food. They bring the nectar back to the hive and put it in the honeycomb. After that, they move their wings very fast to make the nectar cool. Then it turns into honey in the honeycomb.

When bees find nectar, they go back to the beehive and do a special dance. It's called a waggle dance. The dance tells the other bees how much nectar there is, where the nectar is and how far away it is.

When bees leave the beehive to collect nectar, they visit between 50 and 100 flowers. The pollen in the flowers sticks to the bees. The bees take the pollen to other flowers. This is called pollination. Pollination helps flowers make seeds. We need bees to pollinate the flowers of foods that we eat, such as tomatoes, strawberries, beans, apples and a lot of other fruits and vegetables.

3 Read again and complete the chart.

Worker Bee Jobs	Purpose
Build honeycombs	To make honey from nectar
Collect nectar	
Move their wings fast	
Make honey	
Do the waggle dance	
Take pollen to other flowers	

1 **Read and circle the type of text.**

a   a story about ants

b   a text with facts about ants

- Organize your ideas into paragraphs.

- Use a new paragraph for each new topic.

- Use a topic sentence at the beginning of each new paragraph. A topic sentence says what the paragraph is about.

Ants by Alex Bean

Ants are insects. They have six legs and their bodies have three main parts. Most queen ants and male ants have wings.

Ants live in colonies. In some colonies there can be 100,000 ants. Many ants build nests from soil and plants. You can find ant nests in the ground, under rocks or inside plant stems.

Ants have good senses of smell and touch. They use smell to find their nest when they ~~gow~~ go out to look for food. They use touch to communicate. An ant touches another ant's head to give information about food (or danger). Ants don't have ears and they can't hear, but they can feel vibrations in the ground with their feet.

There are a lot of different kinds of ants. Army ants don't build nests. They use their bodies to make a nest. Some ants like fire ants sting. In the rainforest, people sometimes eat lemon ants because they taste good!

Punctuation

Use an apostrophe (') and **s** to show possession with singular nouns.

an ant**'s** nest

2 **Read the text again and answer the questions.**

1   What is each paragraph about?

2   Which ants have wings?

3   Where do ants usually live?

4   How do ants use their senses?

5   Which ants can you eat?

6   Which mistake did Alex make in his text? Why?

3 **Write a text with facts about your favorite insect.**

Phonics
Spellings of the sound /əʊ/

1 **Listen and read. Circle the foods.** 🎧 17

Today is the day of the country show.
You can see things that the farmers grow.
Enormous marrows, tomatoes in rows,
A lot of potatoes in wheelbarrows.

There are fun games to play. Can you throw balls?
You win a prize if a coconut falls.
You can ride on old tractors, see honeybees,
Make some bread dough and try local cheese.

There are natural soaps and pottery bowls.
There are little goats and pretty foals.
There are yellow roses and seeds to sow,
So get your coat! Don't be slow! Let's go!

2 **Read again and write the words with the /əʊ/ sound.**

Honeybees Poster

Materials

★ One sheet of poster board

★ Ruler, pencil and eraser

★ Colored pens and pencils

Stage 1: Plan your project.

1 Work in groups and discuss: How do bees help us have the foods we eat?

2 Honeybees are disappearing. Write your ideas in your notebooks about all the different ways that we can protect them.

Stage 2: Develop your project.

1 Get together with your group. Make a poster to tell people how to help protect honeybees. Look in the library or on the Internet for ideas about which flowers, herbs and plants bees like and where people can plant them in your area. Find information about things that are bad for bees.

2 On your poster, draw the foods that we couldn't enjoy if the bees didn't pollinate the ingredients that are in them.

 Stage 3: Share your project.

1 Attach your group's poster to a classroom wall.

2 Walk around the classroom and look at all the posters.

3 Discuss with your group: How can we protect bees and help them to find nectar and pollinate our food?

Stage 4: Evaluate your project. 🅆🅑 14

Save your *Project Record*. 🖼

★ Read and stick. ✂

Protect the environment where your food comes from.

1 Look and label the pictures.

spider _____ _____ _____ _____ _____ _____ _____

2 Write the answers. What happens if …

1 … there's a moth in your closet?

2 … a wasp is angry with you?

3 … a spider wants to catch flies?

4 … a worm moves through the soil?

5 … bees live in a hive?

3 Read and write the words.

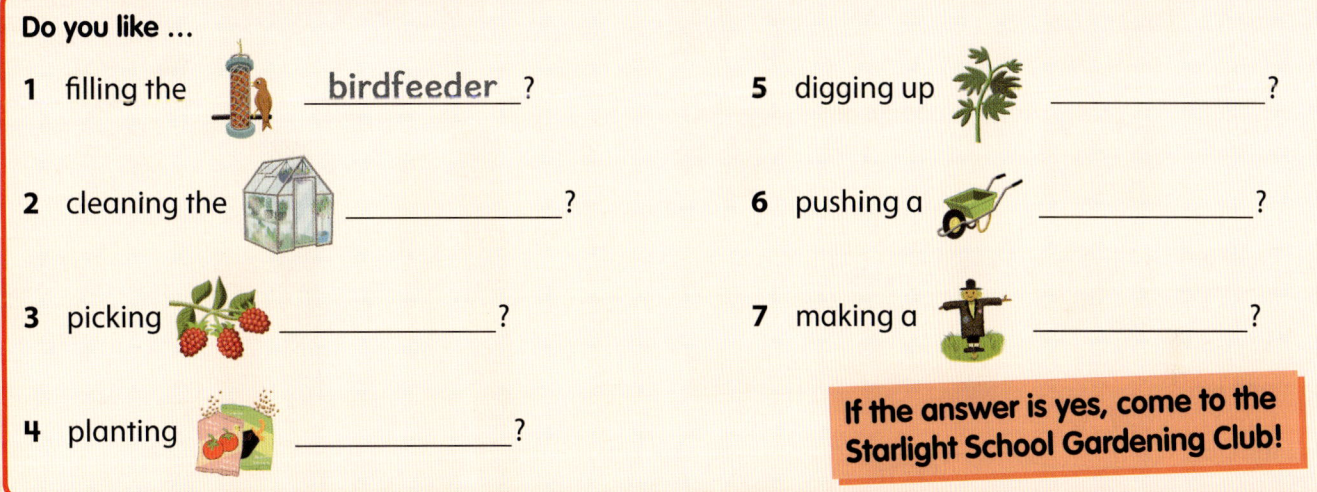

Do you like …

1 filling the ___ birdfeeder ?

2 cleaning the _____?

3 picking _____?

4 planting _____?

5 digging up _____?

6 pushing a _____?

7 making a _____?

If the answer is yes, come to the Starlight School Gardening Club!

4 Complete the sentences with the simple present or present continuous.

1 Look! A spider. It (**make**) is making a web.

2 A centipede (**have**) _____ more than six legs.

3 Only female mosquitos (**bite**) _____.

4 I can see a snail. It (**eat**) _____ that plant.

5 Fireflies (**be / not**) _____ flies. They (**be**) _____ beetles.

6 Look! The moths (**fly**) _____ to the light.

7 Be careful! Wasps (**sting**) _____!

8 Look! Those beetles (**hide**) _____ under the rock now.

Awesome Math homework

Find examples of math in everyday life.

Vocabulary and Reading

1 Match the words with the pictures (1–12). Listen, check and say.

> cartoon   comedy show   commercials   cooking show   documentary   game show
> live sports   music program   soap opera   talent show   the news   the weather

2 Look at Text A. Listen and say the program.

A

CHANNEL **1**	CHANNEL **2**
1 9:00 am Soccer	**8** 11:05 am Love and money
2 11:00 am Cook it!	**9** 12:05 am Win Big
3 11:30 am Ha! Ha!	**10** 12:50 am Top tunes
4 12:30 am Top news stories	**11** 2:00 pm Freddie Five Dollars
5 1:00 pm Today's forecast	**12** WATCH CHANNEL 2
6 1:15 pm African Giants	
7 2:00 pm What can you do?	

B

CLASS 5A WATCH

- comedy shows
- commercials
- documentaries
- cartoons
- the news
- the weather

Number of Students

20

15

10

5

0

TV programs

3 Look at Text B and answer.  1 min

- How many students watch each program?

4 Play *Likes and Dislikes* in pairs.

What do you like watching on TV?

I love the commercials!

5 Read and listen. What is the story about?  20

 The Adventures of Freddie Five Dollars

1 Today I had the most adventurous day of my life!

Wow! What happened, Freddie?

2 Well, it all started in the morning …

I've finished, Grandma.

Thank you, Nathan! Here's $5.00. Keep it safe!

3 But it was a very windy day.

Wow! This is more exciting than Grandma's purse!

4 Unfortunately, I landed in a puddle.

5 It was the most terrifying moment of the day! But the dog took me to a man called Ian.

What do you have there, Sweep? Wow! A five-dollar bill!

Well, I am more intelligent than other dogs!

6 Ian wanted an ice cream.

It's delicious!

Now I can have the most expensive ice cream!

ICE C

7 The ice cream man put me in his pocket. But then a thief saw me.

Stop! Thief!

8 The thief dropped me and then the most surprising thing happened.

Oh no! The police!

9 My five-dollar bill! Great!

And so now I'm safe in Nathan's coin box with you!

 6 Answer in pairs. Use the phrases in the box.

1 Why did Grandma give Nathan five dollars?

2 Why was Freddie scared?

3 Why did the thief take the five-dollar bill?

4 Who was the last person to find Freddie?

I think he / she … because …

I don't think he / she … because …

I agree / disagree because …

Why did Grandma give Nathan five dollars?

I think she gave him five dollars because he did a great job.

1 Look at page 19. Read and listen to the story again. Match the sentence halves. 20

1 Freddie had the most adventurous   a than Grandma's purse.

2 The wind was more exciting   b ice cream.

3 Ian bought the most expensive   c than the puddle.

4 The dog was more terrifying   d day of his life.

2 Complete the chart.

~~colorful~~ delicious Freddie had Ian's ice cream was intelligent

Comparative and Superlative Adjectives with Two or More Syllables							
Comparative				**Superlative**			
Grandma's car was	more	**(1)** colorful	than	other cars.	**(4)** _____	the most	adventurous day of his life.
Ian's ice cream was		**(2)** _____		other ice creams.	When he met Sweep it was		terrifying moment.
Sweep was		**(3)** _____		other dogs.	**(5)** _____		expensive ice cream.

3 Listen and number. 21

Ian's ice cream			Grandma's car		
		 ☐		 1	 ☐

4 Match the words with the pictures of the TV programs.
Describe the pictures in pairs.

boring   educational   entertaining

     exciting   interesting   serious

I think cooking shows are more entertaining than live sports.

I think cartoons are the most entertaining TV programs.

1 **Read part 1 and complete. Read Text B on page 18 again and check.**

1

- (1) _comedy shows_
- commercials
- (2) _cartoons_
- (3) _the weather_

2

We wanted to find out which TV programs the students in our class like and which TV programs the students in our class don't like.

We did a survey and we drew a graph. The graph shows that all of the students in the class like comedy shows and all of the students like cartoons as well.

Most of the students in the class like commercials. Nineteen students like them and watch them. Only one student doesn't like them.

Some of the students in the class like documentaries and the news. Nine students like documentaries, but only three students like the news.

None of the students like watching the weather!

2 **Read part 2 and choose.**

a Part 2 describes a TV program.

b Part 2 describes the students in 5A.

c Part 2 explains the graph.

3 **Match the phrases with the numbers. Read part 2 again and check.**

1 All of the students		**a**	0 / 20
2 Most of the students		**b**	20 / 20
3 Some of the students		**c**	9 / 20
4 None of the students		**d**	19 / 20

4 **Read the survey and choose. Write sentences.**

What kind of movies do you like?

cartoons	25 / 26
comedy movies	26 / 26
romantic movies	0 / 26
scary movies	10 / 26
sad movies	13 / 26
silent movies	0 / 26
documentaries	20 / 26
3D movies	26 / 26

1 (Some) / None of the students like scary movies.

2 All / None of the students like comedy movies.

3 Most / All of the students like cartoons.

4 None / Some of the students like romantic movies.

5 … sad movies.

6 … silent movies.

7 … documentaries.

8 … 3D movies.

1 Look and say what the lesson is about.

2 Listen and repeat. 🎧 22

1	coins
2	bills
3	ten-dollar bill
4	a penny
5	a quarter
6	coin box
7	change purse
8	wallet
9	spend
10	allowance
11	save
12	piggy bank

3 Listen and circle the word. 🎧 23

1 (coins) / bills
2 coin bank / allowance
3 ten-dollar bill / penny
4 allowance / piggy bank
5 wallet / change purse
6 change purse / wallet

 4 Read the advertisements and match them to the meanings.

1 __b__ A man has lost something with money and cards inside.

2 ____ If you buy this item, it can help you save money.

3 ____ You need three quarters and three pennies to pay for this.

4 ____ You can put your holiday coins and bills in here.

5 ____ You need two one-dollar bills to pay for this.

a Ice cream for sale! **Only 78¢!**

b Small brown wallet lost! If found, please call Scot at (327) 598-6241.

c Go-kart rides. $2.00 each!

d Red change purse lost! If found, please call Emma at (327) 562-4113.

e Please give to charity. Money from all countries welcome!

f Do you have an allowance to spend? Then come to World of Fun!

h Newspaper boy / girl needed. Paid $10.00/hour

g This farmyard friend helps you save! Only $4.00!

5 Listen and mark (✔) what the song is about. 🎵 24

☐ saving the allowance

☐ spending the allowance

☐ saving and spending the allowance

6 Listen again and complete the lyrics.

Fold the clothes! Pick up those!
Wash the car! You're a star!
Your **(1)** _allowance_! Here you are!
(2) _____ in your **(3)** _____!
Can you hear the coins clunk?

A **(4)** _____ is one cent,
And a nickel is five,
A dime is ten cents,
A **(5)** _____ is twenty-five,
A one-dollar **(6)** _____,
A five-dollar bill,
(7) _____,
A twenty-dollar bill,
Say please and thanks,
Then put it in your **(8)** _____!

Stores in streets! Buy some sweets!
Ice cream cone! Buy a phone!
Buy a comic, take it home!
(9) _____ money from your coin box,
Can you hear the **(10)** _____ clunk?

[…] Then take it from your piggy bank!

Make the bed! Cut some bread!
Sweep the floor! Clean some more!
Your allowance? Here you are!
Save it in your coin box!
Can you hear the coins clunk?

[…]

7 Circle the options. Which household activities are mentioned in the song?

1 **a** folding clothes
   b washing clothes

2 **a** washing the car
   b washing the dishes

3 **a** making the bed
   b setting the table

4 **a** buying bread
   b cutting bread

5 **a** sweeping the curb
   b sweeping the floor

8 Ask and answer in pairs. 💬

Do you get an allowance?

Yes, I do!

1 Do you get an allowance?
   Yes ➡ Go to question 2
   No ➡ Go to question 3

2 Do you spend it or save it?

3 Do you help in the house?
   Yes ➡ Go to question 4

4 What do you do?

1 Look at the pictures and say what you know about the history of money.

 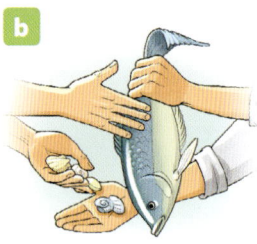   

2 Listen, read and check your ideas. 🎧 25

Today, we use money to pay for goods and services, but where did money come from? Around 9000 BC, people kept farm animals and grew cereals. They exchanged things they had for things they needed. But it wasn't easy to exchange goods. It was necessary to find another person who wanted what you had and had what you wanted. Some goods were difficult to carry and they didn't keep their value. Animals could get old and cereals could go bad. Also, people didn't always agree on the value.

From 1200 to 50 BC, people used small objects to buy and sell goods. Shells, rocks and metal tools were easier to carry. But it was difficult to divide them into smaller amounts and people still didn't agree on their value.

In about 700 BC, the Chinese made the first coins. People could carry coins and they could give other people change. People agreed on the value, because it was written on them. But coins were very heavy and it was possible to steal them.

In the 16th century, people in England gave their heavy gold coins to goldsmiths. The goldsmiths gave them paper receipts to use for money. These receipts were early bills.

Today, we use bills, coins and plastic cards for money. We can spend our money or we can save it to buy things later. It doesn't grow old or rot, it's easy to carry and we can all use it because we agree on its value.

3 Look at the chart and underline more examples of the infinitive of purpose in the text.

Infinitive of Purpose with *to*		
We use money	to pay	for goods.

Adjectives + Infinitive		
It wasn't	easy	to exchange	goods.

4 Read the text again and complete the chart.

Money	9000 BC	1200 to 50 BC	700 BC	Money today
+	People had animals and cereals (1) to exchange .	People used objects (3) _____ and (4) _____ goods.	Coins were easier (6) _____.	Bills, coins and plastic cards are easy (8) _____.
–	It was not easy (2) _____ goods.	It was difficult (5) _____ shells and rocks into small amounts.	It was possible (7) _____ coins.	

5 Say the sentences in pairs.

People had animals and cereals to exchange.

It was not easy to exchange goods.

1 Look and label the coins.

> 1 Indian cent
> 2 one-dollar coin
>   to celebrate
>   Mark Twain
> 3 Peace dollar

 ☐  1  ☐

2 Listen to the dialogue and circle. 🎧 26

1 Where does Lily get her coins from?

   a She buys them with her allowance and people give them to her.

   b She gets them from special magazines.

   c She got them from her grandparents.

2 Which is the most valuable coin?

   a The Indian cent.

   b The Peace dollar.

   c The Mark Twain dollar.

3 Which is Lily's favorite coin?

   a The Indian cent because it's very old.

   b The Peace dollar because it's very valuable.

   c The one dollar silver coin because it celebrates Mark Twain.

3 Underline the words to complete the questions. Listen again and check.

1 **Betty:** _____ coins do you have?

   a What   **b** How many   **c** Which

   Lily: I have 42 coins.

2 **Betty:** _____ do you get them from, Lily?

   a When   **b** Why   **c** Where

   Lily: I save my allowance to buy them. Sometimes people give me coins from other countries, too.

3 **Betty:** Where is this coin _____?

   a made   **b** from   **c** come from

   Lily: It's from the US.

4 **Betty:** _____ is the oldest coin?

   a Where   **b** What   **c** Which

   Lily: This Indian cent is more than 100 years old.

4 Look, listen and repeat. 🎧 27

Perfect Pronunciation

| 100 years old | 1901 | $20 | 1920 | 2017 | 1,000 years old | 1,250 | 3,600 |

5 Complete the pairwork cards. Ask and answer in pairs.

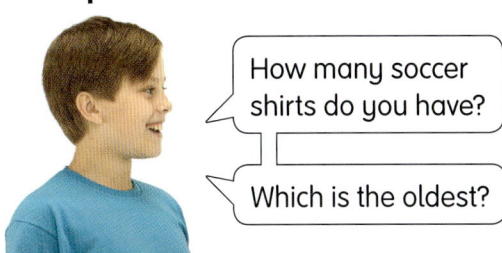

How many soccer shirts do you have?

Which is the oldest?

I have two.

1 Listen and read. Number the pictures.  28

Alex Knows about ...

Using Graphs

Do you know the saying "A picture is worth a thousand words"? This is very true for graphs. Graphs can make it easy to understand information about numbers. Different types of graphs can show information in different ways.

1 We use bar graphs to compare numbers in different groups. You have to read the number where the bar ends to find out the number for a group. This graph shows how many students like doing different activities after school.

a Class 5A: Favorite Activities after school   1

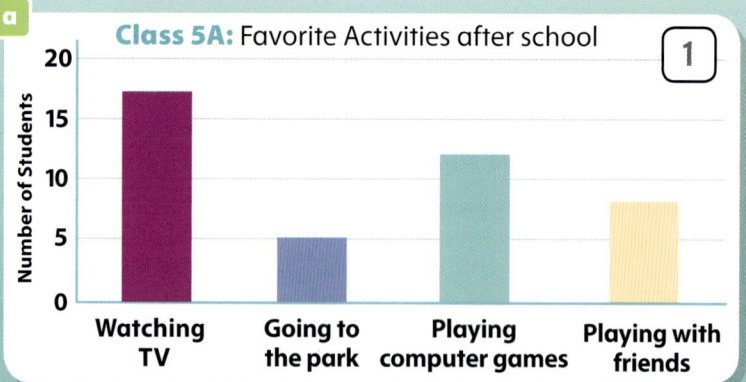

Number of Students: 0, 5, 10, 15, 20

Watching TV | Going to the park | Playing computer games | Playing with friends

b Class 5A: Favorite Activities after school

- Watching TV
- Going to the park
- Playing computer games
- Playing with friends

2 We use a line graph to show information that changes over time. For example, if you want to show what activities a student liked doing last year, and compare it to the activities that they do this year, then you can use a line graph. This graph shows how the activities have changed over time.

3 We use a pie chart to show how each group is a percentage of the total number. Each section, or slice of the pie, shows how big each group is. The pie chart shows the activities that different students in one class like doing. You can see the different percentage for each activity.

c Nathan: Favorite Activities after school

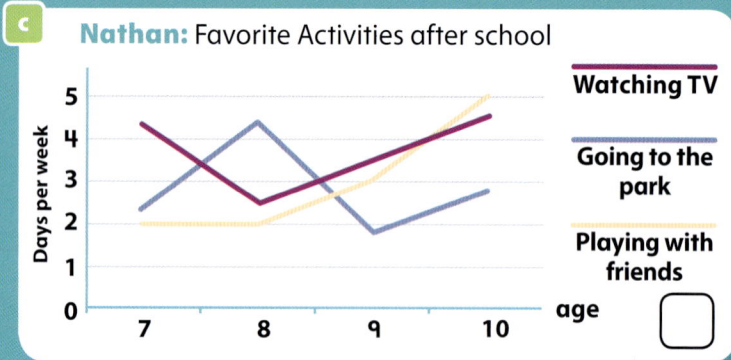

Days per week: 0, 1, 2, 3, 4, 5

age: 7, 8, 9, 10

- Watching TV
- Going to the park
- Playing with friends

2 Look at the graphs again and complete the sentences.

The favorite after-school activities of Class 5A

The favorite after-school activity is **(1)** __watching TV__ .

Playing with friends is more popular than **(2)** _____.

Twelve students like **(3)** _____.

Eight students like **(4)** _____.

The least popular after-school activity is **(5)** _____.

1 **Read the e-mail from Betty. Write an e-mail to Betty and answer her questions.**

- Write what the e-mail is about here.

- Start an informal e-mail with *Hi*, *Hello* or *Dear*.

- A red line shows a spelling mistake in an e-mail.

- You can finish an informal e-mail with your name or the first letter of your name.

From:	bettygreenstreet@nettynet.com
To:	
Sent:	September 14 7:21
Subject:	Friday

Hi Lily,

Can you come to my house on Friday? My mom says it's OK. We can walk home together after school. My house is near the school, so it's easy to get here. My mom says you can stay for dinner. What kind of pizza do you like? We can have cheese and tomato, bacon and mushroom or ham and pineapple. I think ham and pineapple is the most delicious! After dinner, we can watch the nature documentary *Wild*, if you want. But I think the comedy show on Channel 2 is better. It's the funniest show on TV! It's on at 7:15 pm. My mom can take you home at 8 pm when it's finished. Mom says sorry you can't stay the nite this time. It's my grandparents' anniversary on Saturday and we're going to travel to their house early in the morning.

B

P.S. Please bring your nature stickers and we can swap!

Punctuation

Use an apostrophe after plural nouns to show possession.

my grandparent**s'** house

2 **Read the e-mail again and answer the questions.**

1 Who wrote the e-mail?

2 Where can Lily go on Friday?

3 What does Betty want to watch?

4 How long is the comedy show?

5 What does Betty collect?

6 Which spelling mistake did Betty make? Why?

1 **Listen and read. Say the TV programs this person watches.** 🎧 29

If I turn on my TV at home every night,
I can watch boxers box in The Big Fight
Or women on horses and men riding bikes,
And every type of sport that I like.

On TV they show you how to make pies,
What to wear in July and where to buy ties,
How to grow cacti, light a fire in a wood,
Why traveling to islands or Iceland is good.

I watch movies about tigers and spiders and flies,
And birds called red kites that fly high in the sky,
Until Mom says, "Turn it off now! No buts and no whys!
If you watch too much TV, you get very square eyes!"

Phonics
Spellings of the sound /aɪ/

2 **Read again and write the words with the /aɪ/ sound.**

Pie Chart

Materials

★ Two sheets of grid paper

★ Ruler and pencil

★ Calculator

★ Protractor

★ Colored pens and pencils

★ **Read and stick.**

Respect others.

Stage 1: Plan your project. 💬

1   Work in groups. Make a list of your six favorite activities after school.

2   Make a questionnaire. Go around the class and ask every student what they like to do after school. Fill in the questionnaire with the information.

Stage 2: Develop your project.

1   Look at the results of your questionnaire. Count up how many students like to do different activities.

2   As a group, calculate the percentages of each group. For example, if there are ten students who like playing computer games and there are 30 students in the class, then this is the calculation: $(10 \times 100) \div 30 = 33\%$

3   Draw the percentage for each group in the circle. Color each section of the pie chart and label it.

Stage 3: Share your project. 💬

1   Attach your charts to a classroom wall.

2   Present your results to other teams.

3   Discuss with the class. What do most people do after school?

Stage 4: Evaluate your project. 📖 26

Save your *After School Activities Pie Chart*.

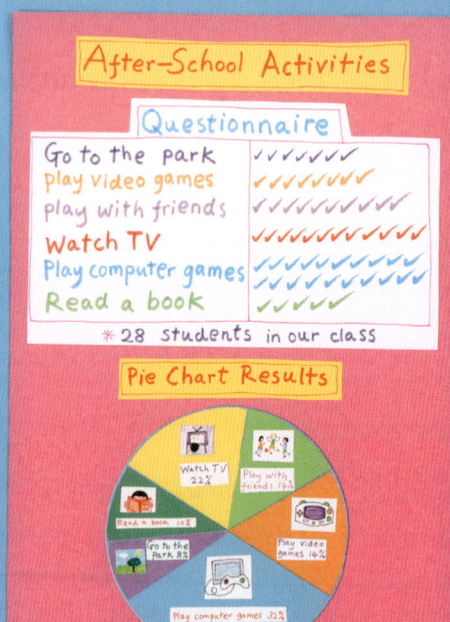

1 **Read the description and write the word.**

1 Men carry their money in this.   w <u>a</u> <u>l</u> <u>l</u> <u>e</u> <u>t</u>

2 This is the name for paper money.   b __ __ __ __

3 Money you get from family members.   a __ __ __ __ __ __ __ __

4 This is the name for metal money.   c __ __ __ __

5 You do this when you go to the store and use your money.   s __ __ __ __

2 **Look and write sentences with comparatives and superlatives.**

	Movie	Price	Minutes	Interesting?
1	Dogs in London	$2.00	120	★ ★
2	Lost in the Mountains	$3.00	100	★ ★ ★
3	The Old House	$1.00	150	★

cheap/expensive   long/short   boring/interesting

1   Movie 1 is cheaper than Movie 2.   4 _____

2   Movie 3 is the cheapest.   5 _____

3   _____   6 _____

3 **Look and write what you can do in town.**

1  Museum

2  Stables

3  Pool

4  Chinese restaurant

5  Ice Rink

6  Movie Theater

You can visit the museum to see old coins.

Heroic History homework

Find out about Ancient Greece.

1 Play *Blockbusters*.

6 ... the most ...

17 ... isn't ...

23 We use ... to ...

1 ... are ...

7 We use ... to ...

12 If ... , the ...

18 ... difficult ...

24 ... more than ...

2 If ... , they ...

13 ... make ...

19 ... aren't ...

3 We use ... to ...

8 ... is ...

14 We use ... to ...

20 If ... , the ...

25 ... easy ...

9 ... eat ...

15 ... are ...

26 ... is ...

4 ... more than ...

10 If ... , the ...

21 We use ... to ...

27 If ... , the ...

5 ... fun ...

11 We use ... to ...

16 ... doesn't ...

22 ... the most ...

Peru

1 Look at the pictures and mark (✔) the topics you think the text will be about.

☐ clothes   ☐ historical places   ☐ sports

☐ bugs   ☐ transportation   ☐ climate

☐ forests   ☐ money

2 Read and number the pictures.

Peru is in South America. The capital city is Lima. Most people in Peru speak Spanish, but many people also speak Quechua and other languages. The Andes Mountains and part of the Amazon rainforest are in Peru.

1 Quechua was the language of the Inca Empire. The Incas lived in the Andes. They were excellent gardeners. People in Peru today still enjoy all the foods the Incas grew. It was very difficult to grow food and build houses there, but the Incas built Machu Picchu over 500 years ago. Machu Picchu is a very famous city. Many thousands of people come to Peru every year to visit Machu Picchu.

2 The Incas kept alpacas. Alpacas are intelligent and calm animals. They live in the Andes and have a thick, soft coat. Alpaca fiber makes warm, soft clothes. It is stronger and warmer than sheep wool. People in Peru make clothes from alpaca fiber. Their traditional clothes are bright and colorful.

3 The Amazon covers more than half of Peru, and it is the biggest rainforest in the world. Scientists think that there are over 2.5 million different types of bugs in the Amazon rainforest. Many of our medicines come from plants that grow there.

Peru also has the largest number of different types of birds in the world. People often visit Peru to enjoy the natural wonders of the Amazon.

3 Read again and complete the chart.

Place	Languages	Historical Site	Natural Site	Animals	Clothes
Peru			The Andes		
Where I live					

31

3 Heroic History

1 Match the words with the pictures (1–12). Listen, check and say. 🎧 30

> bronze   clay   gold   iron   ivory   leather   linen   silver   stone   wax   wood   wool

2 Look at Text A. Listen and say the material. 🎧 31

3 Read Text B and answer. ⏱ 1 min
- Who wrote the diary?
- What is it about?

A

Ancient Greece

3
4
5
6
7
8
9
10
11
12

tablet

abacus

discus

worker

B

Septemvrios 14 800 BC

This morning I went to school with my worker. I can go to school, because my dad is rich. There's one room in my school. We sit on benches. The benches are made of wood. There are twenty boys in my class. My sister wants to go to school too, but she can't. Greek girls stay at home with their moms.

4 Play *Look and Find* in pairs. 💬

> What materials can you see in the class?

> I can see wax … and wood.

c

The Wooden Horse

Many years ago, there was an ancient city named Troy. Troy was on the coast of Asia, across the sea from the Greek city Sparta. For ten long years there was a war between the people of Troy—the Trojans—and the Greeks. The Trojans built a very high wall around their city to protect it. They built gates into the walls and they closed and locked them. The Greeks wanted to enter the city of Troy, but they couldn't. The walls were made of stone and the gates were made of iron, so the city was safe. The Trojans wanted the Greeks to leave, but they didn't. Year after year, the Greeks and the Trojans fought, but year after year neither the Greeks nor the Trojans won the war. Then one day, a Greek general named Odysseus had an idea. The best Greek artists built an enormous horse. The horse was made of wood and it was very beautiful. The Greeks left the horse outside the walls of Troy. Then they sailed away in their ships.

When the Trojan soldiers saw the wooden horse, they were surprised. "Look! It's a horse! It's made of wood." They thought it was a present from the Greeks. They saw that the Greek ships weren't in the harbor and they were very happy. "We won the war!" they said, and they took the horse into their city.

That night the Trojans had a big party. But when the Trojans were asleep, 30 Greeks came out of the wooden horse and opened the gates of Troy. The Greek ships weren't across the sea in Sparta. They were on the coast near Troy. When the gates opened, the Greek soldiers ran into the city and destroyed it. So the Greeks, not the Trojans, won the war.

 6 **Answer in pairs. Use the phrases in the box.**

1 Why didn't the Greeks go into Troy?

2 What did the Greeks make? Why?

3 Why did the Trojans take the horse into Troy?

4 What do you think about the Trojans and the Greeks?

> They … because …
>
> I (don't) think they … because …
>
> I (don't) think they were …
>
> I agree / disagree because …

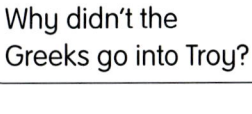

Why didn't the Greeks go into Troy?

I think they didn't go into Troy because of the war.

1 Look at page 33. Read and listen to the story again. Match the sentence halves.  32

1 The wall around Troy   a "It's a big horse and it's made of wood."

2 "What is it?"   b was made of stone.

3 The gates of Troy   c was made of wood.

4 The horse from the Greeks   d were made of iron.

2 Complete the chart.

were   aren't   weren't   ~~isn't~~   wasn't   was

Be made of (Present and Simple Past)

Affirmative	It	's	made of	linen.	It	**(3)** _____	made of	bronze.
	They	're		wood.	They	**(4)** _____		silver.
Negative	It	**(1)** _isn't_		leather.	It	**(5)** _____		gold.
	They	**(2)** _____		iron.	They	**(6)** _____		stone.

3 Listen and number.  33

[ ]   [ ]   [ ]   [ ]   [ ]   [1]

4 Match the words with the pictures. Describe the pictures in pairs.

gold   leather   linen   silver   stone   wood

A long time ago

coins

books

a key

Now

a bridge

a bench

shirts

The book covers were made of leather.

1 Read part 1 and complete. Read Text B on page 32 again and check.

1

Septemvrios 14 800 BC

This morning I went to school with my **(1)** ___worker___ . I can go to school, because my dad is **(2)** _____. There's one room at my school. We sit on benches. The benches are **(3)** _____ wood. There are twenty **(4)** _____ in my class. My sister wants to go to school too, but she can't. Greek girls stay at **(5)** _____ with their moms.

2

At home girls learn cooking and housework. (Boring!) Today we learned reading and writing. I wrote a fantastic, long classical poem on my tablet. My wonderful, old, Greek teacher was very happy. After that we learned arithmetic and I used my new, brown, wooden abacus. My worker watched me. In the afternoon I practiced athletics. I ran, jumped, wrestled and practiced throwing a heavy, round, iron discus. My worker watched me again. It was a cool day!

2 Read and write *rich boys*, *girls* or *workers*. Read part 2 and check.

1 They went to school, but they didn't study.   ___workers___

2 They learned cooking and housework.   _____

3 They learned reading, writing, math and sports. _____

4 They did sports at school.   _____

5 They did athletics at school.   _____

3 Read part 2 again and match.

1	my wonderful	brown	iron	poem
2	a fantastic	round	Greek	discus
3	my new	long	classical	teacher
4	a heavy	old	wooden	abacus

	Opinion	Size / Age / Shape / Color	Origin / Material	Noun
my	wonderful	old	Greek	teacher

4 Describe the people and objects in each picture with three adjectives.

1 Look and say what the lesson is about. 💬

2 Listen and repeat. 🎧 34

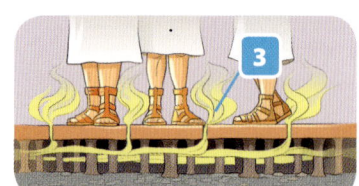

1 couch
2 mattress
3 heating
4 tiles
5 second floor
6 balcony
7 stairs
8 pillar
9 fountain
10 courtyard
11 study
12 mosaic

3 Listen and number the words. 🎧 35

1	couch		fountain		heating
	stairs		study		tiles

 4 Read and complete the sentences with words from Activity 2.
Write the two words from Activity 2 that are not in the text.

I went to Rome and stayed in a beautiful hotel. It looked like an ancient Roman villa.

There were four marble **(1)** _____pillars_____ at the front. In the middle of the building,

there was a **(2)** _____ with a water **(3)** _____. From the courtyard,

there were **(4)** _____ that went up to the bedrooms. My bedroom was on the

(5) _____ and I had a view of the city from my **(6)** _____. My bed had a soft

(7) _____ and there was a comfortable, soft, red **(8)** _____ next to the bed. There

was also a **(9)** _____ in the hotel and people read books or worked there. It had a beautiful

(10) _____ on the floor.

Words not used:

1 _____   **2** _____

36

5 Listen and underline the best title for the song. 🎵 36

Road Builders   The Roman Builders   The Roman Rap

6 Listen again and complete the lyrics.

When you look back in time, in our history,
Tell me who invaded Europe from 200 BC?
They were Romans! They're still really famous.
Romans! Look at what they gave us!
They're the ones who built the roads.

The Romans were builders.
They built big villas,
With **(1)** _tiles on the roof,_
And huge stone **(2)** _____.
In the kitchen it was dark. It was dirty and bare.
But it didn't really matter,
'Cos they only cooked there.
The rich men lay on **(3)** _____
To eat their dinner.
And with so much food, they didn't get thinner.

When you look back in time, in our history …

Now let's take the **(4)** _____ to the
second floor.
Look and see just what those Ancient Romans saw.
In the bedroom was a bed made of wood and leather,
And a **(5)** _____ made of grass
Or straw or maybe feathers.
They had a study with **(6)** _____
floors,
A balcony.
They had a **(7)** _____ with a
fountain and an olive tree.

When you look back in time, in our history …

7 Read the lyrics and write *true* or *false*.

1 The Romans built roofs with stones.   _false_

2 Rich Romans sat at tables to eat.   _____

3 Roman mattresses were made of grass.   _____

4 There was a mosaic on the kitchen floor.   _____

5 The Romans invaded Europe in 200 BC.   _____

6 The Romans built roads.   _____

8 In pairs, compare your house to a Roman house. 💬

My house has a balcony and Roman villas had balconies, too!

Our house doesn't have a study. My mattress isn't made of grass!

1 **Look at the pictures. Say what you know about Roman baths.**

 a

 b

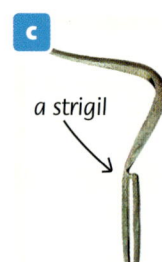 c

a strigil

 d

 e

2 **Listen, read and check your ideas.** 🎧 37

The Ancient Romans <u>used</u> <u>to</u> go to public baths to bathe and to meet their friends. They were very sociable places! The baths had restaurants, games rooms and sometimes libraries.

First, the Romans went into a cold room. Then they went into a warm, dry room and took off their clothes. They used to exercise, and they covered their bodies with perfumed oil. Next they went into the hot room. It was 40°C and very humid. They used to wear wooden sandals because the floor was hot.

They didn't use to scrub with soap. They took the oil and sweat off their bodies with a metal strigil, and then they had a hot bath. Then they used to jump into a very cold pool!

Today, tourists can still see the Roman baths in the city of Bath in England. They can visit the museum and take photographs of the ancient statues. They can see actors in Roman costumes and buy souvenirs in the museum store, too.

3 **Look at the chart and underline more examples of *used to* in the text.**

Used to			
Affirmative	The Ancient Romans	used to	go to public baths.
Negative	They	didn't use to	wash with soap.

4 **Read the text again and complete the table.**

Roman Baths	
Past activities	Present activities
Used to exercise	

- bathe in the baths
- exercise
- take photos
- use soap
- use a strigil
- visit the museum
- jump into cold pools
- buy souvenirs

5 **Make sentences about Romans and tourists in pairs.**

Romans used to bathe in the baths.

Now tourists visit the museum.

1 Look at the price chart. How much did each person spend on their shopping?

THE ROMAN MUSEUM SHOP

		Prices
Toys	Wooden horses	90 cents
	Gladiator puppet	$6.99
	Model villa	$36.50
	Roman kiddie pool	$36.50
Clothes	I ♥ Romans	$15.00
	Cap or hat	$8.00
Special items	Bottle of spa water	70 cents
	Roman baths cup	$4.80
	mug	$5.00

$16.60

2 Listen and number the questions. 🎧 38

☐ How much is that, please?

☐ Do you have any clothes?

1 Can I help you?

☐ Do you sell toys?

☐ What color T-shirts do you have?

3 Look, listen and repeat. 🎧 39

Perfect Pronunciation

We have horses, models, puppets and kiddie pools.
We have T-shirts, hats and sandals.
We have red, black, white, green and gray.

4 Complete the pairwork cards. Ask and answer in pairs. W B 121 💬

Do you sell toys?

Yes, we do. We have puppets, models, balls and computer games.

Lily
Knows about ...

The Rosetta Stone

1 Read and match the descriptions with the pictures. Listen and check. 🎧 40

2

3

1

When we learn about the ancient Greeks, the Romans or the ancient Egyptians, we discover how they changed the world. If we understand languages and we can study objects and buildings from the past, we can learn more about our history.

2 The ancient Egyptians used symbols to write. Symbols are picture words. The name for the ancient Egyptian symbols is hieroglyphics. Hieroglyphics were difficult to write and understand because there were more than 2,000 symbols. Some of the symbols were sounds and some of the symbols were words. They were also difficult because they didn't use any punctuation. So people used an easier way of writing, called Demotic script. About 2,000 years ago, Egyptians stopped writing in hieroglyphics.

Many years later, explorers found hieroglyphic writing in Egyptian pyramids. But they didn't understand it. Many people tried to understand hieroglyphic writing, but it was too difficult. So people didn't know much about life in Ancient Egypt.

In 1799, a French soldier found a special stone in the city of Rosetta. It was a black stone and it had a message on it. The same message was in hieroglyphics, Demotic script and ancient Greek. People understood the writing in ancient Greek and in Demotic script. So they understood what the hieroglyphic symbols on the stone said, too. It took more than 20 years to translate all the thousands of hieroglyphics, but the Rosetta Stone made it easier. The Rosetta Stone was very important because now we understand a lot about life in Ancient Egypt.

2 Read again and complete the timeline. 📝

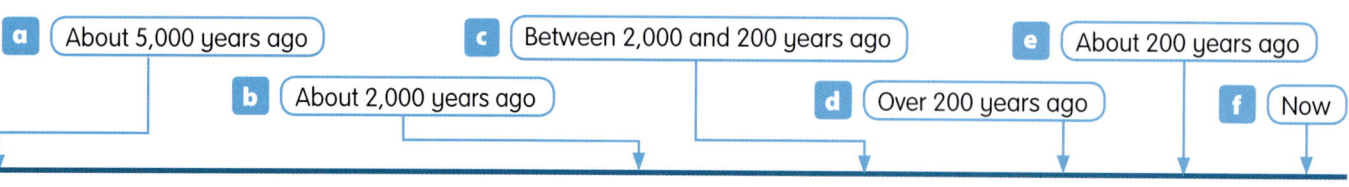

| a | About 5,000 years ago | c | Between 2,000 and 200 years ago | e | About 200 years ago |
| b | About 2,000 years ago | | | d | Over 200 years ago | f | Now |

1 People translated Egyptian hieroglyphics. ☐

2 Egyptians stopped writing in hieroglyphics. ☐

3 Egyptians used hieroglyphics. [a]

4 People didn't understand hieroglyphics. ☐

5 We know a lot about life in Ancient Egypt. ☐

6 A soldier found the Rosetta Stone. ☐

1 **Read the leaflet. What kind of leaflet is it?**

a a history club leaflet   **b** a tourist information leaflet

- Remember to write the opening times, the cost, the location.
- Describe the attraction.
- Include interesting information.
- Write contact details.

VINDOLANDA TRUST
ROMAN ARMY MUSEUM AND ROMAN VINDOLANDA

WHAT IS VINDOLANDA?

Vindolanda is an Ancient Roman site of ten Roman forts. The museum has interesting leather, wood and iron objects and some special 2,000-year-old letters from the site.

It was 73 miles long!

WHAT ELSE IS THERE TO SEE AND DO?

Hadrian's Wall is nearby. Ancient Romans built the wall for Emperor Hadrian from 122 AD to 128 AD.

OPENING TIMES

10 am – 6 pm
(April 1 – September 30)
10 am – 5 pm
(All other times)

ADMISSION CHARGES

Adult	**$6.25**
Child	**$3.75**
Family	**$18.00**
(2 adults and <u>childs</u>)	
Kids' activity sheet	**50¢**

WE ARE HERE!

Punctuation
Only write ¢ for cents when the price is less than one dollar.
25¢ $1.30

2 **Read the text again and answer the questions.**

1 What time does Vindolanda close in June?

2 How much does it cost for two adults and a child?

3 Name three things you can see at Vindolanda.

4 How long was Hadrian's wall?

5 How long did it take to build the wall?

6 Which mistake did Jilly make in the leaflet? Why?

3 **Write a leaflet about your favorite place.**

---

1 **Listen and read. Circle the animals.** 🎧 41

I'm an explorer from Hadrian's Wall.
I see lots of things; some big and some small.
One sheep or two sheep, one deer or two deer,
One leaf over there and two leaves over here.
Sometimes I see geese. Sometimes I see mice.
Sometimes I see wolves and that isn't so nice!
On the ground I find tracks; one fox or two foxes?
And under the ground I find small wooden boxes,
Some scarves for ladies, some big knives for men,
And old, leather sandals for the feet of children.
I eat potatoes and tomatoes for lunch all alone.
I don't see any people until I go home.

Phonics
Spellings of plurals

2 **Read again and write the plurals.**

Monument Poster

Materials

★ One sheet of poster board

★ Scissors and glue stick

★ Pictures of the ancient object or monument you've chosen

★ Colored pens and pencils

  **Anna's Value ...**

★ **Read and stick.**

Be responsible and careful in museums.

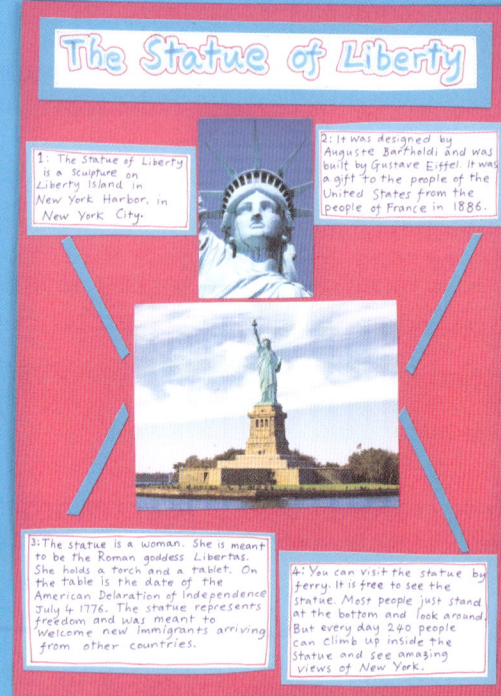

Stage 1: Plan your project.

1 Work in pairs and discuss: What objects or monuments are important in your country?

2 Choose an object, building or monument to investigate.

Stage 2: Develop your project.

1 With your partner, find out as much information you can about your monument, building or object. Think about the following questions: Where and when is it from? What is it made of? Who made it? Why is it important? What does it tell us about life at the time?

2 Cut out pictures of the monument, building or object you chose, or print them from the Internet. Take your poster board sheet and stick the pictures in the middle.

3 Around the outside of the pictures, write information about the monument, building or object.

Stage 3: Share your project.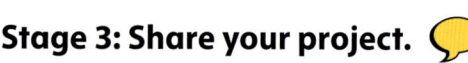

1 With your partner, attach your poster to a classroom wall.

2 Walk around the classroom and look at all the other posters.

3 Discuss in groups. What did you learn from the posters? Why do you think that the objects, buildings or monuments on the posters are important? What have you learned about life in the past?

Stage 4: Evaluate your project.  38

Save your *Project Record*.

1 Look at the picture of the model Roman villa and write the words.

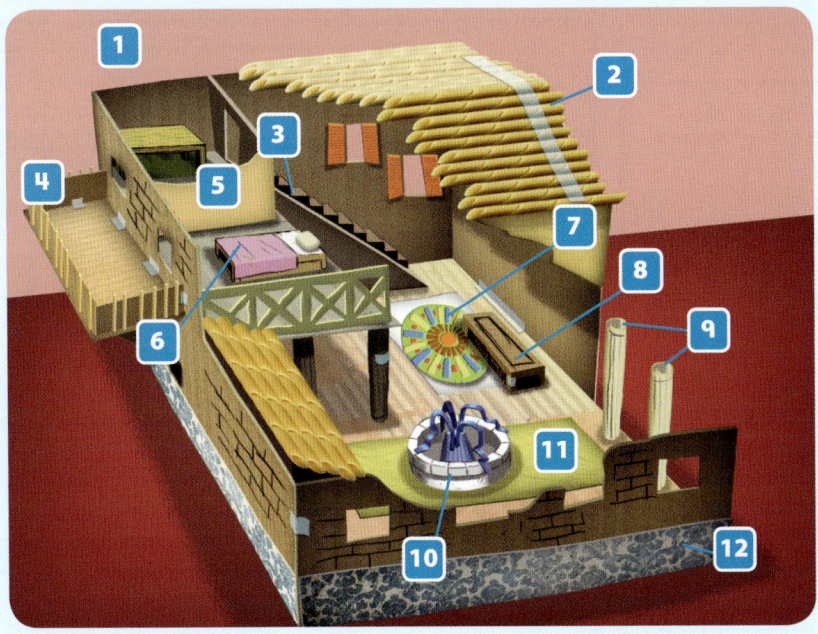

1 ____study____
2 _____
3 _____
4 _____
5 _____
6 _____
7 _____
8 _____
9 _____
10 _____
11 _____
12 _____

2 Read and choose.

In Ancient Rome, a villa **(1) is / was** made of stone.
The model villa **(2) is / are** made of an old cereal box!

In the past, the tiles on the roof **(3) was / were** made of clay, but the tiles on this model **(4) are / were** made of pasta!

3 Complete the text with *used to.*

Class of 1991
Where are they now?

At school, Nigel **(1)** (**be**) __used to be__ very thin.
He **(2)** (**not be**) _____ good at sports.
Now he's very strong. He's a bodybuilder!

At school, Sharon **(3)** (**like**) _____ animals.
She **(4)** (**have**) _____ a cat and a rabbit.
Now she loves animals. She's a zookeeper and she has 26 gorillas!

Great Literature homework
_____

Find out about a famous English writer.

43

A Special Visit

1 Listen and read the story. 🎧 42

1 It's Friday afternoon. Class 5A are practicing for the school Christmas Show.

We wish you a Merry Christmas.
We wish you a Merry Christmas.
We wish you a Merry Christmas
And a Happy New Year!

That's fantastic, 5A! Don't forget to practice at home this weekend!

2

Jump in, kids! We're going to visit Great Aunt Doris in her retirement home.

Yes! Great Aunt Doris!

3

Wow! It's a very big, old, stone house. Look at the pillars.

Why do old people live in a retirement home?

They live here when it's difficult to live at home. Some people are sick and there are lots of carers to look after them.

4

Hello! What a lovely surprise!

How are you, Great Aunt Doris?

I'm doing well. Thank you for coming! It's nice to have a lot of visitors. Most of my friends here don't have many visitors.

5

That's my friend Wilfred. He used to be a gardener. He loves plants and birds, but now he watches game shows all day.

6

And that's Nancy. She used to sing and tell jokes, but now she's very quiet.

7 On Monday at school.

8 The next Saturday

9 In the courtyard.

10 Meanwhile, inside …

11

12

Vocabulary and Reading

1 Match the words with the pictures (1–12). Listen, check and say. 43

> caring   cheerful   energetic   generous   hard-working
> intelligent   lonely   miserable   poor   sociable   stingy   worried

2 Look at Text A. Listen and say the adjective.  44

A

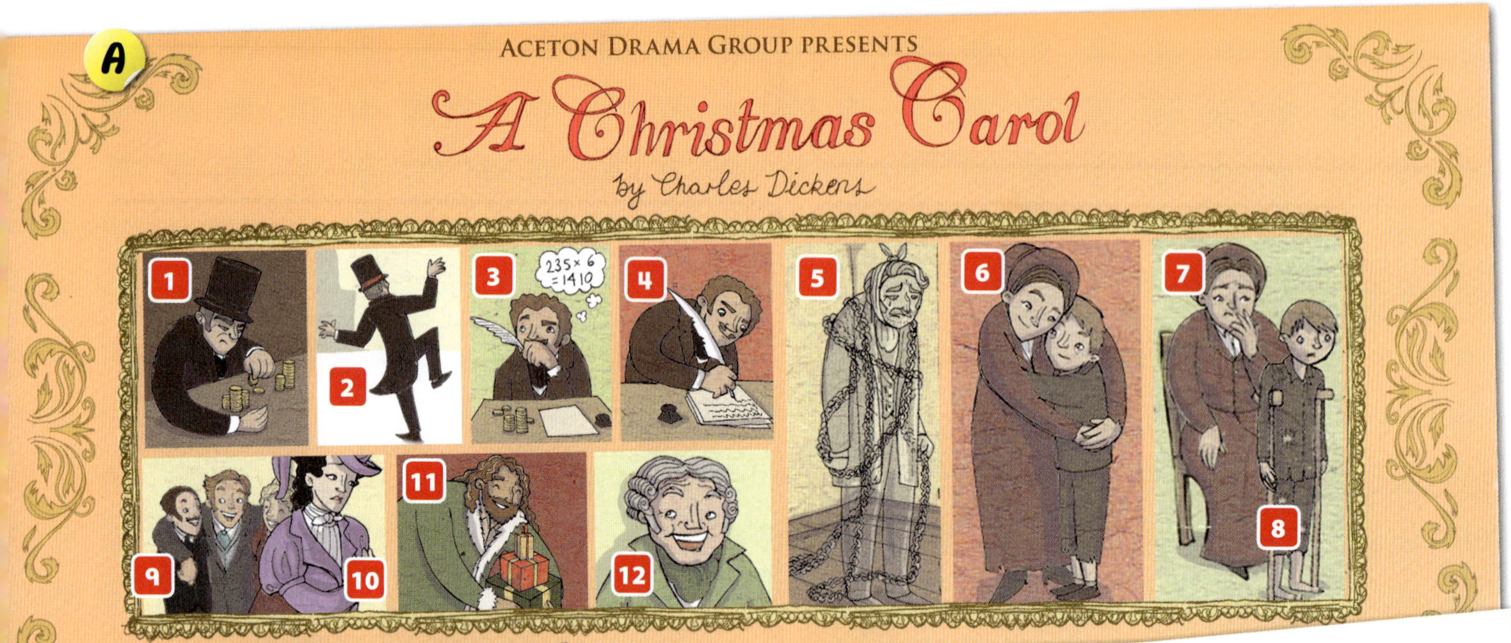

ACETON DRAMA GROUP PRESENTS

A Christmas Carol

by Charles Dickens

1   2   3   4   5   6   7
9   10   11   12   8

THE NEW THEATER, ACETON
DECEMBER 5–15
DOORS OPEN 7 PM

B

Charles Dickens

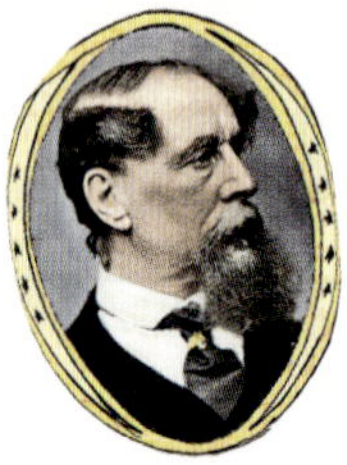

One of the most famous of all English writers, Charles Dickens was born in Portsmouth on February 7, 1812. His parents were John and Elizabeth Dickens. His early childhood was very happy. He went to a good school and he was an excellent student. But when he was 12 years old, his father went to prison because he owed a lot of money to other people. All of Charles' family went to live in the prison apart from Charles. Charles went to live with a family friend called Mrs. Roylance and he worked 10 hours every day at a shoe polish factory.

3 Read Text B and answer.  1 min

- Who was Charles Dickens?
- What was Charles Dickens like as a young child?

4 Ask and answer in pairs.

> What are your family like?

> My mom is kind and hard-working.

c

A Christmas Carol

by Charles Dickens

One Christmas Eve, Ebenezer Scrooge was in his office with his office worker, Bob Cratchit. It was very cold, but Scrooge was a stingy, old man and he didn't want to buy coal for the fire. Scrooge was counting his money when his nephew Fred came in. Fred invited Scrooge to a Christmas party, but Scrooge didn't want to go. Scrooge hated Christmas.

That night, Scrooge was sitting in his armchair at home when he saw a ghost! The ghost was Jacob Marley, Scrooge's old business partner. The ghost said, "Don't be so stingy, Ebenezer! I was stingy like you and now I am unhappy!"

Scrooge fell asleep in his armchair. He was sleeping when another ghost woke him up. "I am the Ghost of Christmas Past," said the ghost. The ghost showed Scrooge his past. He showed him his first job with his generous boss, Fezziwig. He showed him his

fiancée, Belle, who left Scrooge because he loved money too much.

Afterwards, Scrooge felt very sad. He was crying when the next ghost arrived. "I am the Ghost of Christmas Present," said the ghost. The ghost showed Scrooge Christmas Day at Bob Cratchit's house. Scrooge saw that Mr. and Mrs. Cratchit were very poor and their youngest son, Tiny Tim, was very sick. The ghost showed Scrooge the party at Fred's house, too. It was fun and Scrooge wanted to stay, but he couldn't.

Scrooge had one more visitor. He was the Ghost of Future Christmases. He showed Scrooge his grave. People were happy when stingy, old Scrooge was dead. The next morning, Scrooge bought an enormous Christmas turkey for the Cratchit family and he gave Bob Cratchit more money. Then he went to Fred's party. After the visits from the ghosts, Scrooge changed. He was sociable and cheerful, and he was never stingy again.

6 Answer in pairs. Use the phrases in the box.

1 Who is your favorite character? Why?
2 How many ghosts visit Scrooge?
3 How were Jacob Marley and Scrooge similar?
4 How does Scrooge change in the story?

> My favorite … is … because …
> … and … were similar because …
> … changes when …

Who is your favorite character?

My favorite character is the Ghost of Christmas Past!

1 Look at page 47. Read and listen to the story again. Match the sentence halves.

1 Scrooge was counting money

2 Scrooge was sitting in his armchair

3 Scrooge was sleeping

4 Scrooge was crying

a when he saw the ghost of Jacob Marley.

b when the Ghost of Christmas Past woke him up.

c when the Ghost of Christmas Present arrived.

d when Fred came to visit.

2 Complete the chart.

Past Continuous and Simple Past								
Affirmative	It	**(1)** ___was___	snowing	when	she	looked	out of the window.
	He	**(2)** _____	sitting in his chair		he	saw	a ghost.
Negative	She	**(3)** _____	singing		Scrooge	opened	the door.
	They	**(4)** _____	dancing		they	looked	in the window.

3 Listen and number.

4 Match the words with the pictures. Describe the pictures in pairs.
What was everyone doing when Grandma arrived?

___ do homework   ___ paint   _1_ talk on the phone

___ make dinner   ___ play with a ball   ___ sleep

The woman was talking on the phone when Grandma arrived.

1 Read part 1 and complete. Read Text B on page 46 again and check.

1

Charles Dickens

One of the most famous of all English writers, Charles Dickens was born in **(1)** Portsmouth on February 7, **(2)** _____. His parents were **(3)** _____ and Elizabeth Dickens. His early childhood was very happy. He went to a good school and he was an excellent student. But when he was **(4)** _____ years old, his father went to prison because he owed a lot of money to other people. All of Charles' family went to live in the prison apart from Charles. Charles went to live with a family friend called Mrs. Roylance and he worked **(5)** _____ hours every day at a **(6)** _____ polish factory.

2

Charles worked hard, but he hated the factory. It was dirty and there were a lot of rats. After a few months, John Dickens' grandmother died, so he inherited some money. John could pay the money he owed, so the Dickens family left the prison. Charles left the factory, because he could go to school again.

When he left school, Charles worked in an office. He left after a year and a half because he wanted to be a reporter.

His first novel, *The Pickwick Papers*, was published in March 1836, but it wasn't in a book. It was in a magazine. In 1836 he got married and he and his wife, Catherine, had ten children. In his life he published a lot of novels, short stories, plays and non-fiction books too. He died in 1870.

2 Read part 2 and order the pictures (1–6). In pairs, take turns saying what happened in Dickens's life. 💬

 ☐  ☐  ☐  3  ☐  ☐

3 Read part 2 again and write the missing words.

1 John could pay the money he owed, ___so___ the Dickens family left the prison.

2 Charles worked hard, _____ he hated the factory.

3 It was dirty _____ there were lots of rats.

4 He left after a year and a half _____ he wanted to be a reporter.

4 Join and write the sentences. Use *and, but, because* or *so.*

1 Charles Dickens was born in Portsmouth. He moved to London.

2 Charles worked in a factory. His family needed money.

3 Charles' novel was good. A magazine published it.

4 Charles was intelligent. He was a good student.

1 Look and say what the lesson is about.

2 Listen and repeat.

fiction | **non-fiction**

William Shakespeare

1 spy novel
2 graphic novel
3 science fiction novel
4 play
5 ghost story
6 annual
7 manual
8 atlas
9 joke book
10 poetry book
11 recipe book
12 craft book

3 Listen and write the number of the book types you hear. 🎧 48

[ ] atlas   [ ] spy novel   [ ] graphic novel

[ ] play   [ ] joke book   [1] recipe book

4 Write the book types from Activity 2 next to each book title.

1 **Iron Man**

   graphic novel

2 **Maps of the World**

   _____

3 **How to Look after Your Motorcycle**

   _____

4 **Romeo and Juliet**

   _____

5 **The Perfect Spy**

   _____

6 **The Nation's Favorite Poems**

   _____

7 **101 Jokes**

   _____

8 **30-Minute Meals**

   _____

9 **This House is Haunted**

   _____

10 **The President's Year**

   _____

11 **Make Your Own Presents**

   _____

12 **The War of the Worlds**

   _____

Lily's Tune

5 **Listen to the song. Mark (✔) the book types you hear.** 🎵 49

- ☐ annual
- ☐ craft book
- ✔ graphic novel
- ☐ joke book
- ☐ recipe book
- ☐ science fiction

6 **Listen again and complete the lyrics.**

She reads books. She's a reading fan!
Reading fan, reading fan.
She can't write books,
But she knows who can.
I'm a real reading fan.

Shakespeare was a writer
And a clever man.
Stratford-upon-Avon is where he began.
He wrote **(1)** _____poetry_____ and plays and don't forget!
He wrote Romeo and Juliet.
He wrote lots of **(2)** _____,
In the old, old days.
I'm a poetry and William Shakespeare fan.
She's a poetry and William Shakespeare fan.

I can read a __graphic novel__ in one night.
But **(3)** _____ stories really give me such a fright!
I like **(4)** _____ and jokes. Yes, I do.
I like science fiction novels, too.
I read annuals. I read **(5)** _____.
I'm a fiction and non-fiction reading fan.
She's a fiction and non-fiction reading fan.

7 **Read the lyrics and choose the correct answers.**

1 This singer (likes) / **doesn't like** William Shakespeare.

2 This singer **likes** / **doesn't like** poetry.

3 This singer can read a graphic novel in one **week** / **night**.

4 This singer **reads** / **doesn't read** manuals.

8 **Ask and answer in pairs.** 💬

What's your favorite type of book?

I like spy novels best.

1 Look at the pictures and say what you know about Roald Dahl.

2 Listen, read and check your ideas. 50

Roald Dahl, Writer (1916–1990)

Roald Dahl wrote many famous books for adults and children, like *Charlie and the Chocolate Factory* and *Fantastic Mr. Fox.*

Where did Roald Dahl write his children's books?
He wrote his books in a brick hut in the garden of his house. It was white and it had a yellow door.

Which objects did he have in his hut?
He had an armchair, a writing board and a suitcase to put his feet on. He had an electric fire on the ceiling. When it was cold, he sat with his feet in a sleeping bag. He always had chocolate, too. It was one of his favorite foods.

When did he write?
After breakfast in bed, at ten o'clock, he went to his writing hut at ten-thirty every morning. He worked until twelve o'clock and then he went to the house for lunch and a siesta. At four o'clock, he took some tea back to the writing hut and he wrote until six o'clock.

What kind of pencils and paper did he use?
He used yellow pencils and yellow paper. Yellow was his favorite color. The door of his writing hut was yellow, too.

Who did Roald Dahl invite into his writing hut?
Nobody! Roald Dahl didn't want people to go into his hut. Nobody cleaned the hut, so it was very messy! Only the illustrator of his books, Quentin Blake, saw inside the hut.

Why did Roald Dahl send Quentin Blake a sandal?
Roald Dahl sent Quentin Blake one of his sandals because he wanted one of his characters to wear similar sandals. The character was the BFG (Big Friendly Giant). The giant had big boots before, but he looked too scary. You can see the sandal in the Roald Dahl Museum today.

3 Look at the chart and underline more examples of questions in the text.

Simple Past *wh-* Questions	
Who did he invite into his hut?	What kind of pencil did he use?
Who was Quentin Blake?	Which objects did he have in his hut?

4 Read the text again. Complete the questions and match.

1 __When__ did he have breakfast?   **a** In his back garden.

2 _____ color pencils did he use?   **b** At ten o'clock.

3 _____ was his writing hut?   **c** Chocolate.

4 _____ was one of his favorite foods?   **d** Yellow.

5 Ask and answer the questions in Activity 3 and 4 in pairs.

Who did he invite into his hut?   Quentin Blake!

1 Complete the library card for you.

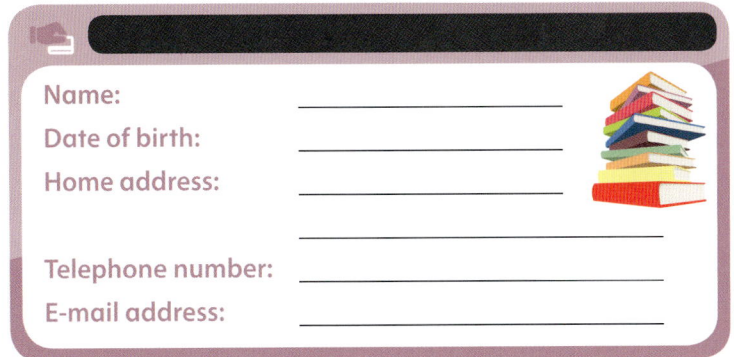

Name: _____
Date of birth: _____
Home address: _____
_____
Telephone number: _____
E-mail address: _____

2 Listen and number the questions. 🎧 51

a ☐ What's your telephone number?

b ☐ Can you spell your last name, please?

c ☐ Do you have an e-mail address?

d [1] What's your name, please?

e ☐ What's your home address?

f ☐ What's your date of birth?

3 Listen again and complete the information.

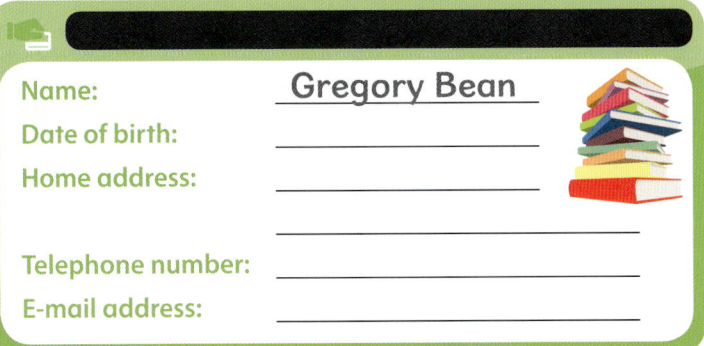

Name: Gregory Bean
Date of birth: _____
Home address: _____
_____
Telephone number: _____
E-mail address: _____

4 Look, listen and repeat. 🎧 52

Perfect Pronunciation

1 a, e, i **2** u, w **3** g, j **4** b, v **5** f, l, m, n **6** q, r **7** x, y, z

5 Complete the pairwork cards. Ask and answer in pairs. 📖 122

Do you have an email address?

Yes, it's adam@tmail.com

Anna Knows about ...

Parts of a Story

1 **Look at the pictures and answer in pairs. What is the story about?**

2 **Listen and read along.** 🎧 53

When we read a story, we can see faraway places, meet amazing people and have a great adventure. A good story is like a delicious cake. You need a few ingredients, and you need to put them together in the right order.

1 Setting. This is the place and time where the story happens. We need to know if the story is in the past, the present or the future. We also need to know where the story happens: in a castle, in a forest or somewhere different.

2 Characters. These are the people or animals in the story. There is often a hero. The hero is the good character. This is the character that you want to be happy at the end. There is often a villain or villains. The villain is the bad character. He or she makes life miserable or difficult for the hero.

3 Plot. The plot is what happens in the story. We need to have these elements in the plot:

- The background. This is often the first thing we read about. This is the history of the characters, their personality and what happened before the story started.

- The conflict. This is often when the hero wants something and the villain wants to stop the hero. The conflict makes the story exciting.

- The turning point. This is when the hero wins. For example, he or she finds the treasure or destroys the villain.

The conclusion is at the end of the story. In the conclusion, we find out what happens to the characters after the conflict and how their lives change.

3 **Read again and complete the chart.**

Jungle Trekking: The Adventures of Sophie Ann		Parts of the Story
Paradise Island		(1) the setting
Sophie Ann		(2) _____
Pirate Dan		(3) _____
The Plot	In Paradise Island animals are free, but pirates arrive to capture monkeys to sell them somewhere else.	(4) _____
	Sophie Ann wants to free the monkeys, but she needs to find Pirate Dan's hidden cave.	(5) _____
	Sophie Ann trips over a tree trunk and finds the map to the cave. She frees the monkeys.	(6) _____
The monkeys are saved. Sophie Ann escapes from the pirates.		(7) _____

1 **Read the review. What kind of review is it?**

a a play review   **b** a film review   **c** a book review

- Write the title of the book.

- Write about: the characters, the background and the setting. Use the simple present.

- Describe what happens in the story. But don't write the WHOLE story!

- Give a recommendation and a rating.

Harry Potter and the Chamber of Secrets **by Alex Bean**

Harry Potter and the Chamber of Secrets is the second story in the Harry Potter series.

The main characters are Harry Potter and his friends, Ron Weasley and Hermione Granger. Harry is starting Year 8 at school, but he doesn't wear a school cap. He wears a school cape! Harry is a wizard and the setting is Hogwarts School of Witchcraft and Wizardry.

At the end of the summer break, Harry has a visit from Dobby, the house elf. Dobby tells him not to go back to school because he is in danger. Harry escapes from his horrible relatives and goes to Ron Weasley's house. Ron and Harry are late for the train to Hogwarts, so they travel by flying car. When they get to school, the adventures begin. Harry, Ron and Hermione find the diary of an old student and together they discover the chamber of secrets.

This book is for everybody who loved the first Harry Potter book! It's fantastic!!

My rating: ★★★★★

Punctuation

We use a comma (,) after introductory phrases that tell us *where*, *when*, *why* or *how*.

At the end of the summer break, Harry has a visit.

---

2 **Read the book review again and answer the questions.**

1 Did Alex enjoy this book? How do you know?

2 What's the setting for the story?

3 Which characters appear in the review?

4 Why does Harry wear a cape, not a cap? What is the difference?

5 What did Harry and his friends find at school?

6 Who would like this book?

3 **Write a review of your favorite book.**

Phonics
Magic E

1 **Listen and read. Where do you find Magic E in a word? What does it do?** 🎧 54

Magic E's a special letter.
Learn it and you spell much better.
A soccer kit becomes a kite,
A little bit is one big bite.
A tiny pin becomes a pine,
A fish's little fin is fine.

Pete is pet without Magic E.
There's no hope! (It's hop, you see!)
Note is not and hate is hat,
Cube is cub and ate is at.
Add an E; make short vowels long.
With Magic E, you can't go wrong.

2 **Read again and write the pairs of words with and without Magic E.**

Story Mini Book

Materials

★ Colored construction paper

★ Colored pens and pencils

★ Self-adhesive tape or stapler

 **Read and stick.**

Take care of books you borrow.

Stage 1: Plan your project.

1 Work in small groups. Think of an idea for a new story.

2 Draw a chart in your notebooks like the one shown on page 54. Think about the parts of the story. Work as a group and write your ideas on the chart.

3 Give your story a title.

Stage 2: Develop your project.

1 Write your story based on the ideas you developed with your group.

2 Fold the colored construction paper and put together the pages of your mini book. Use self-adhesive tape or a stapler to put the mini book together. Write the title of the story and draw pictures to illustrate the front cover of your mini book.

3 Copy your story neatly onto the pages.

Stage 3: Share your project.

1 Swap your mini-book with another group. Read it with your group. Then swap again so you read all the stories in the class.

2 Discuss with your class: Which were your favorite parts of each story? Who was your favorite character? Which ending did you like the best?

Stage 4: Evaluate your project.  50

Save your *Story Mini Book*.

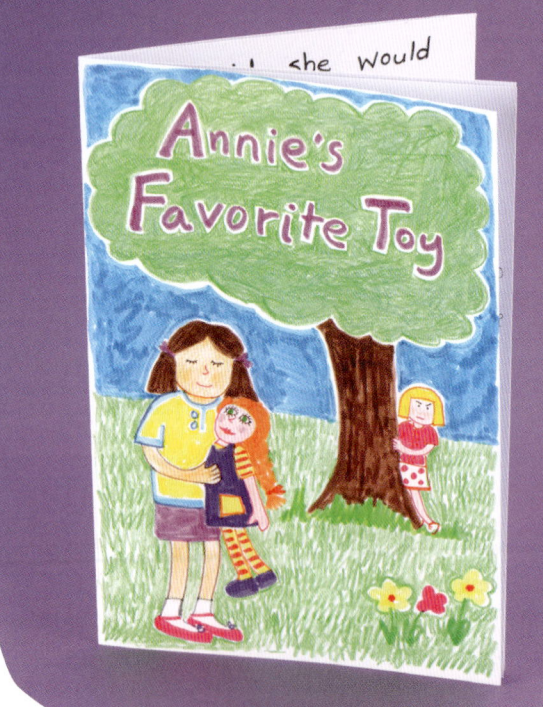

1 **Read and suggest a book type.**

Come to the Starlight School Book Fair at 3:15 pm in the school auditorium. We have a book for everyone!

1 I like scary books.
2 I like learning how to repair things!
3 I like poems and rhymes.
4 I like stories about other planets.
5 I like James Bond books.
6 I like cooking.

1 __ghost story__   3 _____   5 _____

2 _____   4 _____   6 _____

2 **Read and write sentences with adjectives.**

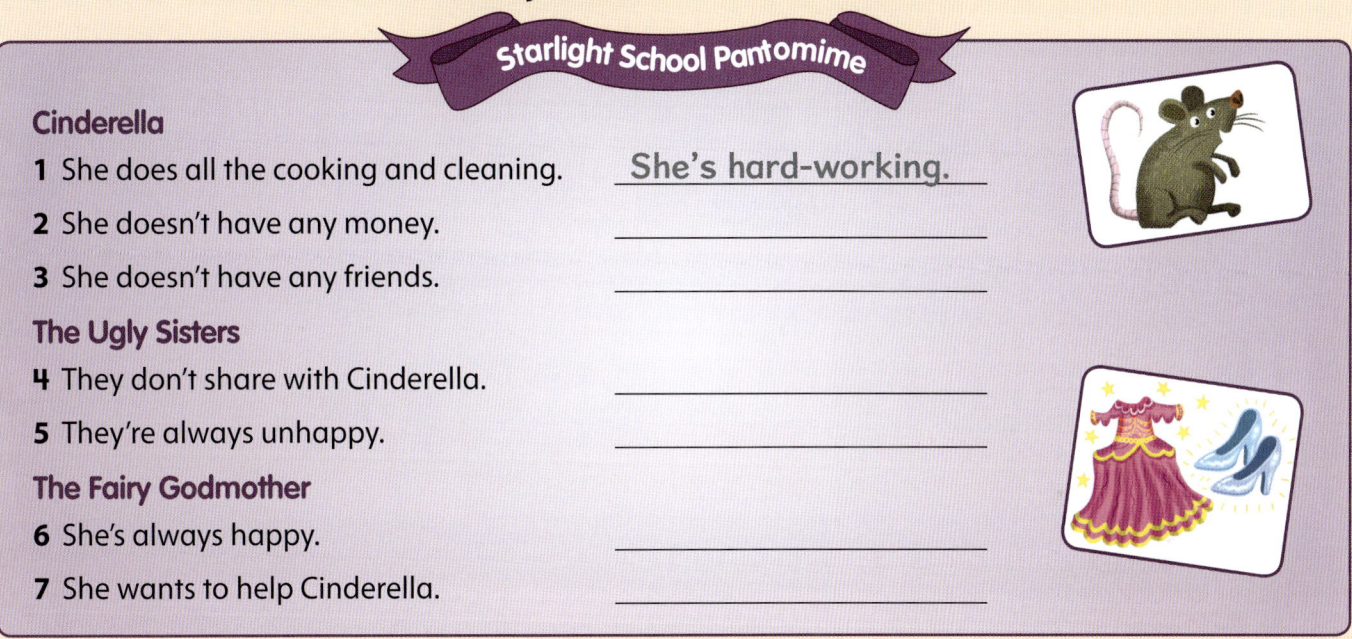

Starlight School Pantomime

Cinderella

1 She does all the cooking and cleaning.   __She's hard-working.__

2 She doesn't have any money.   _____

3 She doesn't have any friends.   _____

The Ugly Sisters

4 They don't share with Cinderella.   _____

5 They're always unhappy.   _____

The Fairy Godmother

6 She's always happy.   _____

7 She wants to help Cinderella.   _____

3 **Complete the questions. Match the questions with the answers.**

what kind of   ~~who~~   what   when

1 __Who__ did the prince marry?
2 _____ did Cinderella leave the palace?
3 _____ vegetable did Cinderella travel in?
4 _____ shoes did Cinderella wear?

a A pumpkin
b Cinderella
c Midnight
d Glass slippers

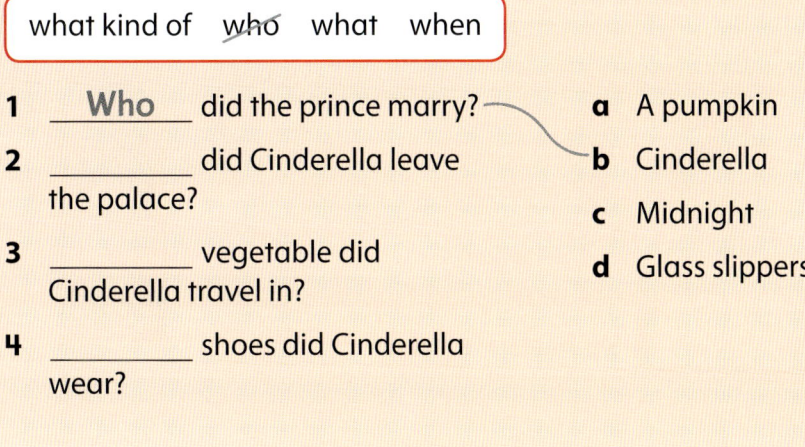

Skillful Sports Homework

Find out about adventure sports.

1 Play *Number Quiz.*

What were the objects made or not made of...

1      **?**

What were the objects made or not made of...

2       **?**

What did your mom/dad/brother/sister/friend use to do or didn't use to do...

3        **?**

What were the people doing when it started to rain at two o'clock ...

4       **?**

What were the people not doing when the phone rang ...

5        **?**

Look and ask questions: What did.../Who did.../Who was.../Which... did...

6       **?**

My points

My partner's points

Mongolia

1 Look at the pictures and circle the best title for the text.

Life in a Mongolian city   **The lifestyle of many Mongolians**   **How to take care of animals**

2 Read and write the title of each paragraph.

Mongolian festival   ~~Nomadic home~~   Nomadic outfit   The importance of animals

Mongolia is a big country in Central Asia. The capital city is Ulaanbaatar. There is the hot Gobi Desert in the south and high mountains in the north. About 40 percent of the people are nomads. Nomads live with their horses, camels, sheep, goats and yaks. Nomads move their home around all year to find grass and water for their animals.

1 _____Nomadic home_____ Nomads live in a big, round, white tent called a ger. It's made of sheep wool and wood. There's a fire in the middle. A ger is easy to take down, put on the back of a camel and take to a different place.

2 _____ Mongolian animals give the nomads milk, meat, leather, wool and transportation. Mongolian nomads are hard-working. They spend all day with their animals. They milk the horses and make cheese and yogurt from the milk. They comb the yaks for their wool. Children look after the animals, too.

3 _____ Mongolian nomads usually wear a deel. It's a long piece of cloth with long sleeves and a belt. It's made of sheep's wool. In winter, they wear a deel made of animal skin. They wear boots made of leather. Their clothes are very colorful and very warm.

4 _____ Every year in July, there is the Naadam Festival, which means "festival of sports." There are three sports: horse racing, wrestling and archery. Nomads are very good at horse racing because they learn to ride as children, and they often win the competitions.

 3 Complete the Venn diagram about daily life.

Mongolia   **Where I Live**

Both
We take care
of animals

5 Skillful Sports

Vocabulary and Reading

1 Match the words with the pictures (1–12). Listen, check and say. 55

bungee jumping   canoeing   karting   mountain biking   mountaineering   rafting
rappeling   scuba diving   skateboarding   skydiving   snowboarding   yachting

2 Look at Text A. Listen and say the sports.  56

A

ADVENTURE SPORTS

Extreme

Water and Ice

Outdoor

B

ACE ADVENTURE CLUB

Are you between 10 and 13 years old?
Do you want to have fun and make new friends this end-of-semester break?
Do you want to try some new, fun sports?

If the answer to any of these questions is **yes**, why not join the Ace Adventure Club?
The Ace Adventure Club offers an adventure every day in a safe and friendly environment.
Contact: aceadventureclub@aceton.com

3 Read Text B and answer.  1 min

- Who is the camp for?
- When is it?

4 Ask and answer in pairs.

Which sports would you like to try?

I'd like to try rafting.

 c

An Incredible Adventure

In November 2008, Jan and Dave Griffith were on a yachting trip with their dog, Sophie Tucker. They were off the coast of Queensland, Australia, when there was big storm and Sophie Tucker fell off the yacht into the sea. At first, Jan and Dave hoped to find their dog. They looked for her for an hour, but the weather was very bad and they couldn't see her. Finally, they decided to continue their journey. They were very sad, because they thought their pet was dead.

But Sophie Tucker wasn't dead. She managed to swim to St. Bees Island. This was incredible because it was more than five miles to the island and there were a lot of sharks in the sea! St. Bees Island has rainforests and grasslands and not many people. When some local people saw Sophie Tucker, they thought she was a wild dog. She looked very thin and sick, and she didn't want to take food from people.

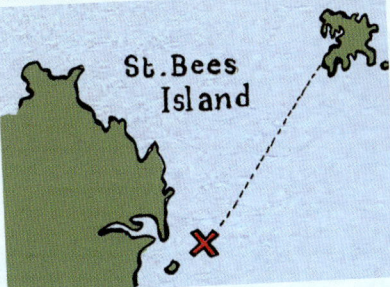

But Sophie Tucker wanted to survive. She learned to hunt koalas and baby goats on the island. Soon she was strong and healthy again. Jan and Dave heard about the dog on the island, but they didn't think the dog was Sophie Tucker. Sophie Tucker lived on the island for four months. Then one day. local people found some dead goats. They told the wildlife rangers to come to the island and they asked them to catch the dog. The people helped the rangers find Sophie Tucker.

The rangers took the dog to the mainland by boat. They invited Jan and Dave to come to the port to check. When Jan and Dave saw the black and gray dog on the boat, they couldn't believe it. It was Sophie Tucker! They called their dog and she ran to them. She was very excited to see Jan and Dave, and they were very happy to have their pet again. Sophie Tucker's incredible adventure was over!

 6 **Answer in pairs. Use the phrases in the box.**

1 Why did the dog fall into the sea?

2 Why was the dog's journey to the island difficult?

3 How did the dog survive on the island?

4 Who does the dog live with now?

> Because of …
>
> Because he / she / it / they …
>
> I (don't) think they …

Why did the dog fall into the sea?

Because of the storm!

1 Look at page 61. Read and listen to the story again and order the sentences.

a ___ She learned to hunt koalas and goats.

b ___ Jan and Dave hoped to find their dog.

c ___ She didn't want to take food from people.

d _1_ Sophie Tucker fell into the sea.

e ___ Sophie Tucker managed to swim to the island.

f ___ They decided to continue their journey.

2 Complete the chart.

Verb Patterns with Base Forms							
Verb + base form with *to*			**Verb + object + base form with *to***				
Jan and Dave	hoped		find their dog.	The people	told	the rangers		come to the island.
They			continue their journey.	The people		the rangers	to	catch the dog.
Sophie Tucker		to	swim to the island.	The rangers		Jan and Dave		come to the port.
She			hunt goats.				
She			survive.				

3 Listen and number.

Come to the island.

4 Tell the story in pairs.

1 Tim / learn / scuba dive.

2 He / decide / go to Ecuador. He / hope / see / dolphins. BUT HE LOST HIS BOAT!

3 He / manage / swim to / an island.

4 A girl found Tim! / Zoe / help / Tim / get back to the mainland.

5 Tim / invite / Zoe / to dinner. Then / he / ask / Zoe / marry him.

Tim learned to scuba dive.

He decided …

1 **Read part 1 and complete. Read Text B on page 60 again and check.**

1

ACE ADVENTURE CLUB

Are you between 10 and (1) ___13___ years old?
Do you want to have fun and make new (2) _____ this end-of-semester break?
Do you want to try some new, fun (3) _____ ?

If the answer to any of these questions is (4) _____, why not join the Ace Adventure Club?
The Ace Adventure Club offers an adventure every (5) _____ in a safe and friendly environment.
Contact: aceadventureclub@aceton.com

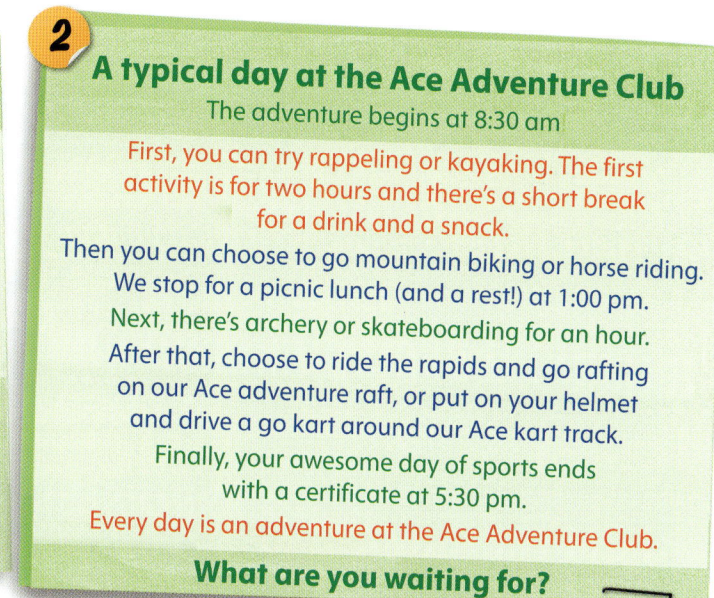

2

A typical day at the Ace Adventure Club
The adventure begins at 8:30 am

First, you can try rappeling or kayaking. The first activity is for two hours and there's a short break for a drink and a snack.
Then you can choose to go mountain biking or horse riding. We stop for a picnic lunch (and a rest!) at 1:00 pm.
Next, there's archery or skateboarding for an hour.
After that, choose to ride the rapids and go rafting on our Ace adventure raft, or put on your helmet and drive a go kart around our Ace kart track.
Finally, your awesome day of sports ends with a certificate at 5:30 pm.
Every day is an adventure at the Ace Adventure Club.

What are you waiting for?

2 **Read part 2 and mark (✔) the activities you can do at The Ace Adventure Club.**

 a ✔
 b
 c
 d
 e
 f

3 **Complete Anna's diary about her day at the Ace Adventure Club.**

> Then   After   ~~First~~   Finally   Next

This camp is so cool! Today we did a lot of activities. **(1)** ___First___,
I tried rappeling. We were very high up and it was scary!
(2) _____ I went mountain biking. We had a race down a
hill and I won. (Hurray!) **(3)** _____, we had a picnic lunch in
the sun. **(4)** _____ that I did skateboarding, but I wasn't very
good at it. (Lily was fantastic!) **(5)** _____, I went rafting in the
Ace Adventure Raft. I fell in the river! It was fun!

4 **Write about Martin's day at the Ace Adventure Club.**

 a
8:30 am
 b
11:00 am
 c
2:00 pm
 d
3:00 pm
 e
5:30 pm

1 Look and say what the lesson is about. 💬

2 Listen and repeat. 🎧 59

1 parachute
2 harness
3 rope

4 goggles
5 jumpsuit

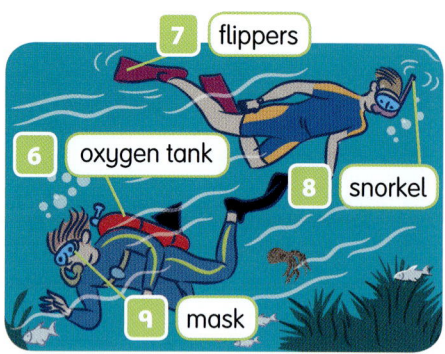
7 flippers
6 oxygen tank
8 snorkel
9 mask

10 life jacket
11 seat belt

12 paddle

3 Listen and write the number of the matching picture. 🎧 60

a 【4】 b 【 】 c 【 】 d 【 】 e 【 】 f 【 】

4 Look and complete the mind map with words from Activity 2.

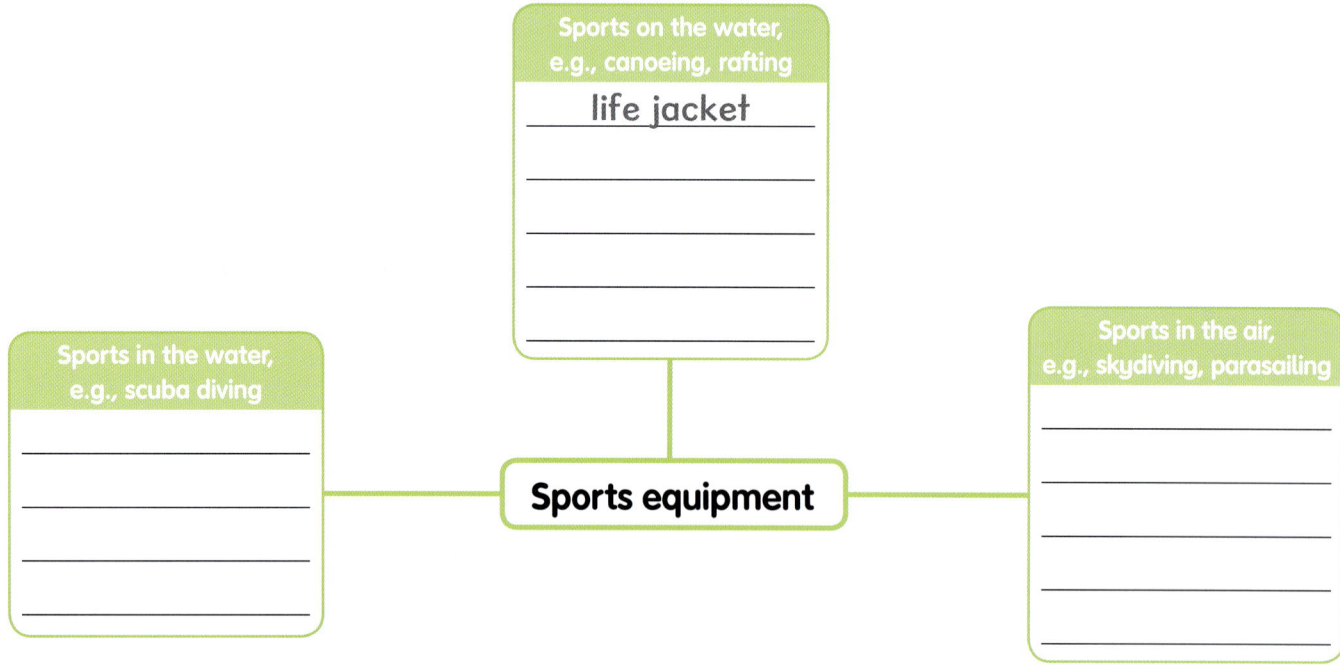

Sports on the water,
e.g., canoeing, rafting

___life jacket___
_____
_____
_____
_____

Sports in the water,
e.g., scuba diving

_____
_____
_____
_____

Sports in the air,
e.g., skydiving, parasailing

_____
_____
_____
_____

Sports equipment

5 Listen to the song. Mark (✔) the sports equipment you hear. 🎵 61

- ☐ flippers
- ✔ life jacket
- ☐ paddle
- ☐ goggles
- ☐ mask
- ☐ parachute

6 Listen again and write the missing sports equipment.

Come on get your coat,
Here's the boat on the river.
Jet boating is for me!
It's alright! Hold on tight!
Now the sun is shining bright.
Put your **(1)** ____seat belt____ and
(2) _____ on!

Let's jet boat together.
It's wet and it gets wetter!
Yachting is good fun,
Jet boating is better.
In and out of canyons,
In boats upon the river.
I love adventure sports!

Look up there! Do you dare
Jump from planes into the air?
Skydiving is for me!
Don't forget your **(3)** _____,
Skydive **(4)** _____ and jumpsuit.
Fly high but don't land in a tree!

Let's all go skydiving!
It's scary. It's exciting.
It's more fun than golf,
More extreme than kung fu fighting.
High above the land,
In the sky between the clouds.
I love adventure sports!

7 Match the lyrics that rhyme.

1 It's alright! Hold on tight!
2 It's wet and it gets wetter!
3 Don't forget your parachute,
4 It's scary. It's exciting.

a skydive goggles and jumpsuit.
b More extreme than kung fu fighting.
c Jet boating is much better.
d Now the sun is shining bright.

8 Think of an adventure sport. Play a guessing game in pairs. 💬

Do you need goggles?

No, you don't.

Do you need a life jacket?

Yes, you do.

1 **Look at the pictures and say what you know about indoor climbing.**

2 **Listen, read and check your ideas.** 62

A climbing wall is an artificial wall to practice rock climbing. Some climbing walls are outdoors, but most are indoors in fitness centers. A P.E. teacher at Leeds University in England made the first climbing wall in 1964. He put pieces of rock into a corridor wall.

Today most climbing walls are made of wood or brick. The walls have handholds and foot holds. These are different colors to show different climbing routes.

Lead climbing is a style of rock climbing with two people. The lead climber climbs up the wall with a rope. He or she has to wear a harness. The other climber must hold the rope at the bottom for safety.

Bouldering is a style of rock climbing without a rope. The climbers must wear rock-climbing shoes, and they have to climb over a crash pad so they don't hurt themselves if they fall. Some climbers use chalk to make their hands dry. They don't have to use chalk, but it helps them climb.

Climbers don't have to be adults. Children can use climbing walls too, but they have to follow the safety rules. They mustn't climb without a helmet, and they mustn't climb directly under another climber.

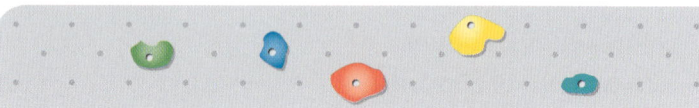

3 **Look at the chart and underline more examples of modal verbs in the text.**

Modal verbs of obligation		
Have to and *must* = necessary	*Mustn't* = not permitted	*Don't have to* = not necessary
The lead climber has to wear a harness.	They mustn't climb without a helmet.	Climbers don't have to be adults.
The other climber must hold the rope.		

4 **Write sentences about climbing.**

> Bouldering climbers   Lead climbers   Climbers   Children

1 wear a helmet
   __Children must wear a helmet.__

2 have a rope

3 use chalk

4 wear climbing shoes

5 hold the rope for safety

6 follow safety rules

5 **Say more sentences about climbing in pairs.**

> Climbers have to climb over a crash pad.

> Climbers don't have to wear sun hats or caps.

1 Ask and answer in pairs. What do you do on the weekend?

2 Listen and mark (✔) the diary that shows when William and Anna decide to meet. 63

1

Saturday Morning	Sunday Morning
Saturday Afternoon	Sunday Afternoon **skateboarding**

☐

2

Saturday Morning	Sunday Morning **skateboarding**
Saturday Afternoon	Sunday Afternoon

☐

 3 Listen again to the conversation. Write the letter.

William: Hi, Anna! Do you want to come to the skate park with me on Saturday morning?

Anna: (1) ___D___

William: Oh, OK. Can you come on Saturday afternoon then?

Anna: (2) _____

William: I have to do my homework on Sunday morning, but I'm free after lunch.

Anna: (3) _____

William: OK! See you at the skate park!

A That sounds great, but I play soccer on Saturday mornings.

B I'm free on Sunday afternoon, too. I can meet you at two-thirty.

C I'm sorry. I'm going to the movie theater. Do you want to come?

D I'd like to come, William, but I have a soccer game on Saturday morning.

E Yes, I'm free. When do you want to meet?

F Sorry, I can't. Alex, Lily and I have tickets for the movie theater on Saturday afternoon. What about Sunday?

4 Look, listen and repeat. 64

Perfect Pronunciation

Do you want to come to the skatepark?

Can you come on Saturday afternoon?

Alex, Lily and I have tickets for the movie theater.

I have a soccer game on Saturday.

I can meet you at two-thirty.

See you at the skate park!

5 Complete the pairwork cards. Ask and answer in pairs.  123

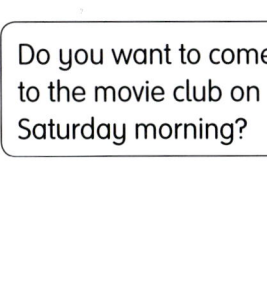

Do you want to come to the movie club on Saturday morning?

Sorry, I can't. It's my mom's birthday.

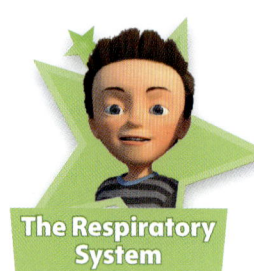

The Respiratory System

1 **Match the heading with the paragraph.** 🎧 65

a Where does the oxygen go?

b How do we breathe?

c Why does our body need oxygen?

d What happens when we breathe out?

The respiratory system is the part of our body that lets oxygen into our body. We can't live without oxygen. We breathe to get oxygen from the air.

_____

When we eat food, we get energy. But oxygen helps the body burn the energy so we can use it to move and to live.

a

We breathe oxygen into our mouth and nose. It goes down the trachea. The trachea is about 10 centimeters long and carries oxygen into our lungs. We have two lungs. The lungs have very thin walls. The oxygen goes through the walls into the blood. The blood carries the oxygen to the heart, and the heart pumps the blood with the oxygen to all the different parts of the body.

_____

When the body burns energy, it makes carbon dioxide. It's very bad for the body. It's important to let the carbon dioxide out of the body. So the blood carries the carbon dioxide from the different parts of the body back to the lungs. Then we breathe it out.

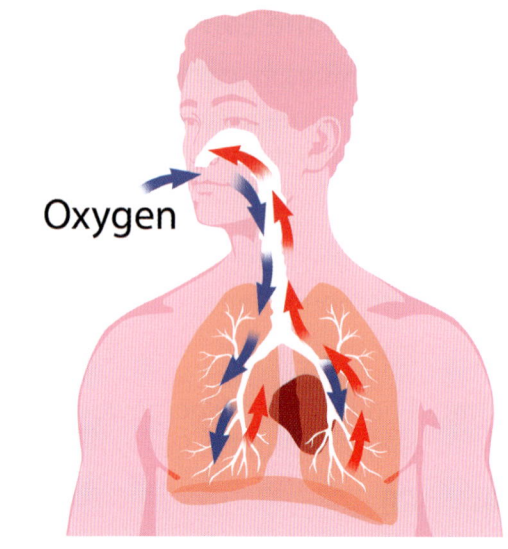

Oxygen

_____

Below your lungs there is the diaphragm. The diaphragm is a big muscle. When you breathe in air, the diaphragm gets flat and moves down. This gives your lungs more space to breathe in more air. When we breathe out air, the diaphragm moves up. This pushes the air out of the lungs.

2 **Read again and complete the flow diagram.**

First, oxygen in the air goes into the mouth / nose.

⬇

_____
_____

⬇

The oxygen goes into the blood, then into the heart. Next, it goes around the body.

➡

_____
_____

_____
_____

⬆

The blood carries the carbon dioxide back to the lungs.

1 Read the adventure story. What kind of ending does it have?

a a funny ending   **b** a happy ending   **c** a sad ending

- At the beginning of the story, write where and when the story takes place, who the characters are and how the characters are feeling.

- In the middle, use the past continuous to describe background actions and the simple past to describe the main events.

- At the end of the story, write what happened and how the characters felt.

The Canoe Ride by Anna Bean

João lived in a small village in the Brazilian rainforest. One day, he had to go to the nearest big town with his mother and father. They got into their canoe on the river. It was early in the morning and João was still sleepy.

The family was traveling fast down the river, when the canoe motor suddenly fell off the back of the canoe and into the water. João's father shouted, "Oh no!" He was very worried. He couldn't control the canoe without the motor and there were no paddles. The canoe was still moving quickly and they all knew there were waterfalls further down the river. João's mother was very ~~afrade~~ afraid.

Suddenly João had an idea. There were no paddles in the canoe, but there was a rope. When they were passing a big tree, he threw the rope. The first time he missed the tree, but the second time he managed to catch one of the branches. His mother and father helped him hold the rope and the boat stopped. After that, they used the rope to pull the canoe to the side of the river. They were very happy to be safe on land again.

Punctuation

Use a comma before the direct speech.

Use speech marks around the direct speech.

He shouted, "Oh no!"

2 Read the adventure story again and answer the questions.

1 How many characters are in the story?
2 Where were the characters going?
3 Why was it dangerous to continue with no motor?
4 How did João stop the canoe?
5 How did the characters feel at the end of the story?
6 Which mistake did Anna make in her story? Why?

3 Write an adventure story.

1 Listen and read. Circle an activity in each verse. 🎧 66

Here's the story of Mavis and Dave.
They're super sporty and very brave.
They both had a smile on their face,
When they met at a cheese rolling race.

Mavis and Dave are never afraid.
So Dave found a trip, booked it and paid.
They waited for a train to Spain.
Then they sailed in a yacht in the rain.

As Dave's birthday was a special day,
They went parasailing by the bay.
Mavis shouted, "Well, this is great!
But I hope my harness doesn't break!"

Phonics
Spellings of the sound /eɪ/

The next day they joined a group of eight.
Luckily they were all the right weight.
One by one they jumped out of the plane.
Then they flew back up and jumped out again.

2 Read again and write the words with the /eɪ/ sound.

69

Breathing Rate Line Graph

Materials

* Classroom clock with second hand
* Ruler and pencil
* One sheet of grid paper

 **Read and stick.**

Exercise to keep your body healthy.

Stage 1: Plan your project.

1 Work with a partner. Choose an exercise that makes you breathe fast, for example running or skipping.

2 Make a chart that records the number of breaths in a minute before the exercise, during the exercise and one to three minutes after the exercise.

3 Take turns doing the experiment. Count each other's breaths before, during and after the exercise. Write the numbers in the chart.

Stage 2: Develop your project.

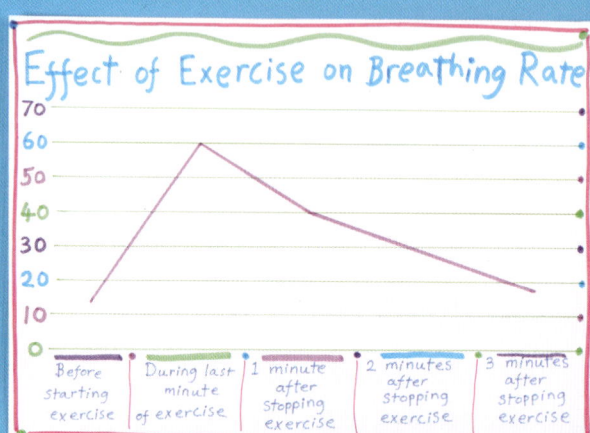

Effect of Exercise on Breathing Rate

1 Draw a line graph to show how the number of breaths every minute changes.

2 Write the times along the line going across the bottom. Write the number of breaths along the line going up to the top. Start the numbers at 10 and finish them at 70.

3 Compare and contrast your results with your partner.

Stage 3: Share your project.

1 Attach your line graphs to a classroom wall.

2 Present your results to other teams.

3 Discuss with the class: What happens to your lungs when you exercise? How does exercise keep your body healthy?

Stage 4: Evaluate your project.  62

Save your *Breathing Rate Line Graph*.

1 Look and write the rules.

Starlight Soccer Team Rules

1 (wear / a T-shirt)   You must wear a T-shirt.
2 (wear / soccer boots)   _____
3 (wear / shin pads)   _____
4 (wear / dirty tennis shoes) _____
5 (bring / a drink)   _____
6 (kick / the ball at the wall) _____
7 (wear / shorts)   _____

2 Read and write the adventure sports.

Starlight School parents do the scariest things!

I have to wear a helmet and a harness, but I don't have to wear a jumpsuit. I don't jump out of planes; I jump off high bridges.

Mrs. Julia Greenstreet

Sometimes I have to use a rope and wear a helmet. I always wear warm clothes and walking boots.

Mr. Gregory Bean

I can wear any clothes and I don't have to wear a helmet, but I have to wear a life jacket. I need ropes for my sport and a yacht, of course!

Chris Bedding

1 ____bungee jumping____   2 _____   3 _____

3 Read and write the missing words.

invited   helped   managed   ~~decided~~   wanted   told   hoped   learned

Dear Class 5A,

I am on vacation in Austria. When I arrived, I **(1)** __decided__ to have ski lessons. I **(2)** _____ to ski quickly and I **(3)** _____ to ski down the highest slope. Then I **(4)** _____ to try another winter sport. Some friends **(5)** _____ me to go snowboarding. I **(6)** _____ to snowboard for two days, but I broke my leg on the first morning! My friends **(7)** _____ me to get down the mountain. I went to the hospital and the doctor **(8)** _____ me not to do any more sports. Oh no!

Your school secretary, Miss Click

Amazing Art homework

Find out about street art.

71

6 Amazing Art

1 Match the words with the pictures (1–12). Listen, check and say. 🎧 67

> clothes pin   drill   fridge   iron   light switch   needle
> plug   saw   teapot   thread   toaster   vacuum cleaner

2 Look at Text A. Listen and say the everyday object. 🎧 68

Sculpture by Paul Cox

3 Read Text B and answer. ⏱ 1 min

- What object is described in the text?

4 Play *Find It Out* in pairs. 💬

> What's it for?

> You use it to make holes.

B MY TRIP TO LONDON
BEAN, JANET
Sent: September 8 7:23
To: Lily Bean
Attachments: Amazing sculpture!

Hi Lily,
Aunt Janet here! I'm sending you a photo for your art homework. It's an enormous street art sculpture I saw in London yesterday. I saw it in the daytime, but at night it can light up. The sculpture is 4.6 meters wide and two meters high. The main part of the sculpture looks like plastic, but it isn't plastic. It's made of wood. At the moment it's green, but it isn't always the same color. The paint and the lights change color.

5 Read and listen. Mark (✔) the picture of the WEEE Man. 69

c

The Story of the WEEE Man

Our reporter has traveled to Cornwall to say Happy Birthday to the WEEE Man!

The WEEE Man is a sculpture. He's called the WEEE Man because he's made of old machines people don't want, or WEEE (Waste Electrical and Electronic Equipment).

In 2004, the Royal Society of Arts (RSA) wanted to teach people about WEEE. They wanted to show how much electrical equipment people waste in their lifetime. They decided to build a sculpture and they asked an artist called Paul Bonomini to design it.

Paul created an enormous robot and in April 2005, British people saw the WEEE Man for the first time. The sculpture is 7 meters tall and it weighs 3.3 tons. This is the same amount of WEEE the average British person throws away in their lifetime.

The average person throws away 5 fridges, 3 washing machines, 8 toasters, 8 irons, 35 cell phones, 8 computers, 4 keyboards, 23 keyboard mice and 6 TVs!

First the WEEE Man stood outside City Hall in London, but he's now at the Eden Project in Cornwall. Today is his fifth birthday. A lot of people come to see the sculpture every year.

"I've come to see the WEEE Man because we've just done a project about recycling at school," says schoolboy Jack Taylor. "I made a model of a WEEE boy! I used food cans."

His schoolmate Tara Smith adds, "I haven't made a model, but I've painted a picture of the WEEE Man. I think he's really cool!"

"I've visited the WEEE Man lots of times," says Mary Magee from Oxford. "I've just taken lots of photographs to show my grandkids. The WEEE Man is very important because it has taught people about recycling."

Her husband Bob Magee adds, "I've just thrown away an old radio! But now that I've seen the WEEE Man, I understand that we shouldn't waste so much."

That's right! Thank you, WEEE Man! We've learned a lot from you!

6 Answer in pairs. Use the phrases in the box.

1 Why is the WEEE Man in the news?

2 Who built him and why?

3 What is he made of?

4 What do visitors to the WEEE Man learn?

He's in the news because …

… built … because …

They learn that …

Why is the WEEE Man in the news?

He's in the news because …

1 Look at page 73. Read and listen to the story again. Match the sentence halves. 🎧 69

1 Mary Magee

2 The WEEE Man

3 Jack Taylor

4 Bob Magee

a has taught people about recycling.

b has just thrown away an old radio.

c has just taken a lot of photographs.

d has just finished a school project about recycling.

2 Complete the chart.

Present Perfect (*have* + past participle)								
Affirmative					Negative			
He	has	(just)	**(1)** painted	a picture.	She	hasn't	**(4)** _____	a project.
They	have		**(2)** _____	a photograph.	They	haven't	**(5)** _____	to the Eden Project.
			(3) _____	the WEEE Man.				

3 Listen and number. 🎧 70

4 Describe and guess the pictures in pairs. 💬

1

separated items for recycling / not taken the boxes to the recycling center

2

looked at some paintings / not looked at the sculptures

3

finished a painting / not put her paints away

4

finished her water / not recycled the bottle

5

taken a photo / not printed it

6

started a craft project / not finished it

He has started a craft project. He hasn't finished it yet.

It's number 6!

1 Read part 1 and complete. Read Text B on page 72 again and check.

1

MY TRIP TO (1) _____London_____
BEAN, JANET
Sent: (2) _____ 8 7:23
To: Lily Bean
Attachments: Amazing sculpture!

....

Hi Lily,
Aunt Janet here! I'm sending you a photo for your art homework. It's an enormous street art sculpture I saw in London yesterday. I saw it in the daytime, but at (3) _____ it can light up. The sculpture is 4.6 meters wide and (4) _____ high. The main part of the sculpture looks like plastic, but it isn't plastic. It's made of (5) _____. At the moment it's (6) _____, but it isn't always the same color. The paint and the lights change color.

2

Today I went to Covent Garden. It's a famous part of London with a market, shops, restaurants and the Royal Opera House. Covent Garden often has street performers and I listened to a girl playing a violin. She was very skillful and the music was fantastic. I spoke to a cheerful artist, too. She was painting a woman on a bicycle. There was a strong smell of coffee in the square, so I went to a café for breakfast. Afterwards I walked around the market. It has a large glass roof and it's very beautiful. I bought a book about London with lots of colorful photos. The book has been very useful because the weather has been awful this afternoon! I've stayed in the hotel and I've almost finished my book. It's almost dinner time now!

Aunt Janet xx

2 Read part 2 and say what Aunt Janet did in London. Match the pictures with the adjectives.

1  **2**  **3**  **4**  **5**

____ cheerful   ____ skillful   ____ beautiful   ____ colorful   **1** useful   ____ awful

3 Describe the pictures using adjectives with *-ful*.

1  **2**  **3**

4 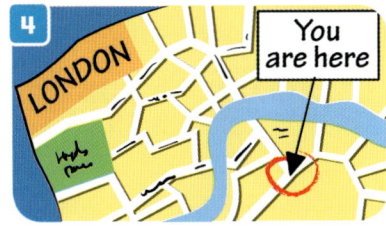 **5**  **6**

1 Look and say what the lesson is about. 💬

2 Listen and repeat. 🎧 71

1 wide

2 spiky

3 round

4 dirty

5 clean

6 flat

7 shiny

8 dull

9 bumpy

10 dry

11 wet

12 narrow

3 Listen and match the opposites. Write the two missing words from Activity 2. 🎧 72

A wide   B shiny   C clean   D wet   E flat

1 round   2 dirty   3 dull   4 narrow   5 dry

Missing adjectives: _____ , _____

4 Complete the sentences with adjectives from Activity 2.

1 The statue is made of bronze. When the sun shines on it, it looks gold and _____ **shiny** _____ .

2 The sculptures were of people, but the people were very thin. Their bodies were very _____ .

3 The sculpture was made of stone. It wasn't shiny. It was gray and _____ .

4 Close your eyes and touch the sculpture of the tree. It feels like a real tree—bumpy and _____ .

5 There were lots of bird droppings on the statue. It was very _____ .

6 It rained a lot and all the sculptures were very nice and _____ .

5 **Listen to the song. Mark (✔) the names of sculptures that you hear.** 🎵 73

- [✔] *The Angel of the North*
- [ ] *The Circle of the Sea*
- [ ] *The Tree of Remembrance*
- [ ] *The Light of the Sky*
- [ ] *Afloat*

6 **Listen again and complete the song.**

There are sculptures of queens.
There are sculptures of kings.
The Angel of the North
Has amazing **(1)** ___wide___ wings.
54 meters wide,
And 20 meters tall,
He stands high on a hill,
Looking down over all.

Some sculptures are special.
Some sculptures are plain.
They're **(2)** _____ *in the sun.*
They're **(3)** _____ *in the rain.*
Some sculptures are heavy.
Some sculptures are light.
Some sculptures have water,
Some light up at night.

There are sculptures with names.
Like the names on this tree.
The Tree of Remembrance
Should remind you and me.
Pretty leaves, silver leaves,
They're **(4)** _____ and they're **(5)** _____.
When the birds sit up there,
People look at that.

Some sculptures are **(6)** _____.
Some are high off the ground.
Afloat is a sculpture
That is turquoise and **(7)** _____.
Can you see the sea through
The hole in the middle?
It's near to the beach.
It's big. It's not little.

[...]

7 **Read the lyrics and circle the answers.**

1 *The Angel of the North* is … meters tall.
  a 54   **b** 20 ⟵(circled)

2 *The Angel of the North* is …
  a in a wood.   **b** on a hill.

3 *The Tree of Remembrance* is made of …
  a silver.   **b** bronze.

4 *The Tree of Remembrance* has …
  a pretty flowers.   **b** shiny leaves.

5 *Afloat* is …
  a square.   **b** round.

6 *Afloat* is near …
  a a river.   **b** the sea.

8 **Find some objects. Play a guessing game in pairs.**

It's round and smooth. It's shiny.

Is it the apple?

1 **Look at the pictures. Say why the knitting is there.**

2 **Listen, read and check your ideas.**

Knit the City is a group of four knitters <u>who</u> leave their knitting in public places in London and call it "yarnstorming." Deadly Knitshade (not her real name) started the group in 2009.

Where was the first yarnstorm?
The first yarnstorm was in London, in Covent Garden, where we covered a wooden barrier with colorful knitting.

Do you always knit covers for things?
No, we knit lots of different things, from fruit to pirates.

Which knitted thing is your favorite?
My favorite is the biggest thing I've knitted, a squid called Plarchie, which is made out of 160 plastic bags. It's 8 meters long.

Is yarnstorming difficult?
Sometimes. We hung knitted hearts from a statue called Eros in London, which is 7 meters above the ground. It was very high up, and it was very windy. Some people clapped when we managed to do it.

Do people take your knitting?
Yes, but that's OK. We yarnstorm and then we take photographs. After that, people can take the knitting. Once I got a photograph from a man who took a knitted cat for his living room. Another man took a knitted mushroom, which he gave to his daughter.

Do you only yarnstorm in London?
Well, we have just been to Berlin, in Germany, where we left knitted sausages, so one day we might come to your city, too!

3 **Look at the chart and underline more examples of relative pronouns in the text.**

Relative pronouns (*which, who, where*)		
It's a squid	which	is 8 meters long.
I got a photograph from a man	who	took a knitted cat.
We have been to Berlin,	where	we left knitted sausages.

4 **Read the text again and match the sentence halves.**

1 There are four knitters — leave their knitting in public places.
2 Eros is a statue — he gave to his daughter.
3 A man took a knitted mushroom, — who — took a knitted cat for his living room.
4 Deadly Knitshade got a photo from a man — which — they covered a wooden barrier with knitting.
5 Plarchie is a squid — where — is 7 meters above the ground.
6 The first yarnstorm was in Covent Garden, — is made from 160 plastic bags.

5 **Say the sentences in pairs.**

Plarchie is a squid …

… which is made from …

1 Look at the pots and label them with the adjectives below.
   Add some other adjectives of your own.

| beautiful   sky blue   brown   gigantic   skillful   bright   dreadful   orange |

1

sky blue
_____
_____

2

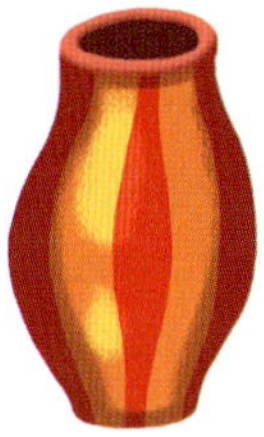

_____
_____
_____

3

_____
_____
_____

2 Listen to the dialogue. Match the children and the pots they made. 🎧75

   [1] Lily   [ ] Alex   [ ] Anna

3 Listen again. Read and mark (✔) the phrases you hear.

   1 [✔] What a fantastic exhibition!

   2 [ ] That's wonderful! Good job!

   3 [ ] You've done a lot of preparation!
           Congratulations!

   4 [ ] I like your pot, Lily.

   5 [ ] Good work! You're very skillful!

   6 [ ] Lily! That's amazing. I love it!

   7 [ ] Isn't the color beautiful, Lily!

   8 [ ] It's gigantic!

   9 [ ] Wow! It's a very interesting pot.

   10 [ ] You've worked hard.

4 Look, listen and repeat. 🎧76

Perfect Pronunciation

| fantastic | terrific | gigantic | dramatic |
| exhibition | congratulations | preparation | description |

5 Complete the pairwork cards. Ask and answer in pairs. [WB] 124 💬

What a fantastic plate!
The color is awesome!

Thank you! I'm glad
you like it!

79

Lily Knows about ...

Sculpture

1 **Listen and read along. Label the pictures.** 🎧 77

Sculptors are artists who make sculptures. There are sculptures in museums which are over 20,000 years old. A sculpture can show us what is important to a person or a culture. It can also make us think about something in a different way.

There are different techniques to make a sculpture.

- In modeling, a material is built into a sculpture. Modeling uses soft materials, for example, clay, plaster or wax. The sculptor adds more and more of the material to make the sculpture. A famous example of this is the *Chinese Terracotta Army*. This is a group of about 8,000 clay soldiers and horses. They are all different. About 700,000 people made these sculptures over 2,000 years ago.

- Carving uses materials like stone, marble or wood to make sculptures. The sculptor has a big piece of the material, then carves bits away until the sculpture is ready. *David,* by Michelangelo, is a famous example of carving. It is made of marble.

- Casting is when a liquid material is put into a container in the shape of the sculpture. The liquid material gets hard. We can use casting to copy a sculpture. For example, there are about 25 copies of the famous, bronze sculpture *The Thinker*, by Auguste Rodin. They are all over the world.

- Constructing is a new type of sculpture. It uses a lot of different materials and puts them together. *Long Term Parking*, by Arman, is a sculpture in Paris. It is nearly 20 meters high and over 6 meters wide. It has many old French cars in concrete.

1 **2** **3** **4**

Chinese Terracotta Army _____ _____ _____
_____ _____ _____

 2 **Read again and look. Complete the chart.**

Sculpture	Technique	Material(s)	Description
The Terracotta Army	modeling	clay	Lots of different people
David			
The Thinker			
Long Term Parking			

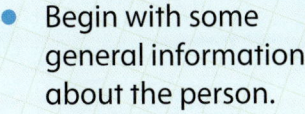

1 **Read the description. It is a description of Mr. Bean's …**

a character   **b** appearance   **c** character and appearance

- Begin with some general information about the person.

- Describe the person's physical appearance.

- Describe the person's feelings and their personality and character.

- You can describe some of the things they usually do, too!

My Photograph by Lily Bean

This photograph is of my dad, who is called Gregory. He's 37 years old and he works in a secondary school, where he's a math teacher.

My dad has short, straight, chestnut brown hair, which is a little bit spiky. He has a mustache and a small beard, and he has dark brown eyes and big eyebrows. He has fair skin, but he doesn't have freckles. He sometimes wears glasses, but he isn't wearing glasses in my photograph. He's wearing a clean, blue and white shirt.

In my photograph, Dad looks tired, because it's 6 o'clock and he's just gotten home from work. Normally he's very active and lively. He likes running and he rides a mountain bike too school! He looks a bit grumpy in the photograph, too! He isn't normally grumpy. He's very cheerful and he tells us funny stories. My dad is also very clever. He can repair teapots, irons and toasters. He just repaired the vacuum cleaner!

Punctuation
Use an apostrophe between **o** and **clock** in times.
6 o'clock

2 **Read the text again and answer the questions.**

1 What is Mr. Bean's first name?

2 What is his job?

3 What does he look like?

4 How does Lily describe her Dad's character?

5 What everyday objects does Lily write about? Why?

6 Which mistake did Lily make? Why?

3 **Write a description of your friend.**

---

1 **Listen and read. Circle the animals.** 78

Phonics
Spellings of the sound /uː/

Sue was an artist.
She worked in a zoo.
She drew animals,
And made models, too.
She worked through the night
With scissors and glue.
In her artist's room,
She knew what to do.

Sue drew a blue goose,
A few cockatoos,
An emu, a moose
And two kangaroos.
She wore uniforms,
And super new boots.
The birds flew to her,
But the monkeys threw fruits.

2 **Read again and write the words with the /uː/ sound.**

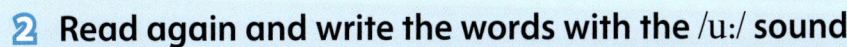

A Sculpture

Anna's Value ...

Materials

★ Objects to make a sculpture
★ Colored paint
★ Brushes
★ Glue

 Read and stick.

Be kind to your friends and show respect for their work.

Stage 1: Plan your project.

1 Work in small groups. Think about ideas for a sculpture. It can be an object such as a building or an animal, or something more abstract such as family or the environment.

2 Decide how you are going to make the sculpture and what materials you will use.

3 Draw a picture of how your sculpture will look when it is finished.

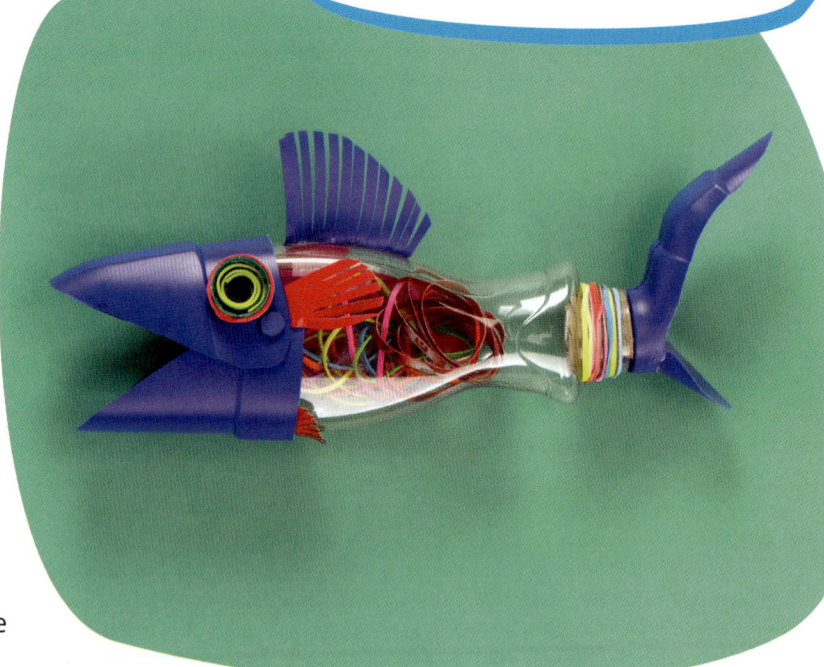

Stage 2: Develop your project.

1 Collect all the materials that you are going to use.

2 Glue or tie your materials together in the shape that you want, or paint or stick other materials onto it.

Stage 3: Share your project.

1 In your groups, present your sculpture to your class. Tell the class what your sculpture is about and what materials you used to make it.

2 Discuss as a class: Why is it important to show respect for other people's work?

Stage 4: Evaluate your project.  74

Save your *Project Record*.

1 **Look and write the names of the everyday objects.**

1	_____teapot_____
2	_____
3	_____
4	_____
5	_____
6	_____
7	_____

2 **Look at the sculpture. Write sentences to describe it.**

1 _This is a sculpture of an animal._

2 _____

3 _____

4 _____

5 _____

3 **Read and write *where*, *who* or *which*.**

Trip Report by William Victory

Last week we went to Liverpool, **(1)** ___where___ we
visited the Tate Gallery. We went with Miss London,
(2) _____ has been there before. We saw
paintings by René Magritte, **(3)** _____ was an
artist from Belgium. My favorite painting was Galconde,
(4) _____ he painted in 1953. It shows a city
(5) _____ men are falling from the sky. I'm
painting a similar picture for the art competition,
(6) _____ is next week.

Fun Geography
homework

Find out about the
Arctic.

83

1 Play *Battleships.*

What are their vacation plans?	What are the rules of sports? Use *have to*, *must*, *musn't*, or *don't have to*.

What did the teacher do?	Say the sentence.	Complete the sentence.

	A	B	C	D	E
1	Max/hope to	Amy/decide	Rosie/manage	Sophie/learn	Jack/want
2	He/invited/Jenny	He/told/Henry	He/asked/Mia	He/helped/Lucas	He/told/the class
3					
4	Milo/paint	I/just/finish	Ben/not/do	Freya/just/visit	Katie/not/recycle
5	It's a ...	He's a ...	We went to a ...	I visited ...	It's a ...

Namibia

1 Look at the pictures. What do you think is special about Namibia? Circle the words.

the art   (the coast)   the food   the houses   the mountains   the sand dunes
the sports   the transportation   the tribes

2 Read and answer the questions.

1 Why don't many people live in Namibia?   The land is too dry.

2 Why is the Skeleton Coast dangerous?   _____

3 Why do people visit Sossusvlei?   _____

Namibia is in the south of Africa. The capital city is Windhoek, which means "windy corner." There are about 30 languages in Namibia. Most people speak English and Afrikaans. Namibia is famous for its wild animals, dangerous coast and high sand dunes.

Many different tribes live in Namibia, and they all wear different clothes, eat different food and have different cultures. Some are nomads and keep animals. Others have farms and grow crops. Namibia is a big country, but not very many people live there because people can only grow crops on 10 percent of the land. The rest is too dry—it is difficult to survive. The coast of Namibia is called the Skeleton Coast. It is called this because people used to hunt whales in Namibia and many whale bones used to come up on the beach. It is also called the Skeleton Coast because the weather is often very foggy and lots of ships crashed into the rocks. People come to surf here, but you have to be a very good surfer, as it can be very dangerous.

The Namib desert is partly in Namibia. It is a coastal desert and is more than 2,000 kilometers long. Some people think the Namib is the oldest desert in the world. It has very high sand dunes. People go to a place called Sossusvlei to hike up to the top of the sand dunes and then surf down. It takes two hours to walk to the top of the highest dune at Sossusvlei, and it takes five minutes to surf down.

 3 Read again and complete the chart with special features. 📝

Special features	
Namibia	**Where I live**
Sand dunes	

The Spring Fair

1

Hello! You three are very cheerful this afternoon!

Yes, it's the school Spring Fair on Saturday. We love the fair!

Here's an invitation for you and Dad.

The Starlight School invites you to
A Spring Fair
Saturday May 1 – 2 pm to 5 pm
Traditional dancing · Skateboarding
Second hand clothes and books · Go Karting
Ice cream and smoothies · Costume competition

Raffle: 1st Prize: Fridge
2nd Prize: Vacuum Cleaner   3rd Prize: Toaster

2

We all have to help at the fair. I'm going to help Miss Sporty to teach skateboarding.

That's very energetic, Lily! Can I learn to skateboard?

No problem, Dad!

3

I've decided to make smoothies with William.

When did you learn to make smoothies, Alex?

It's easy! We have this recipe book, which we found in the school library.

Blueberry smoothie
Ingredients
- 175 ml apple juice
- 120 ml natural yogurt
- 1 banana
- 170 g blueberries

Method
1 Put all the ingredients into a blender and blend until smooth.
2 To serve, pour into tall glasses.

4

I'm hoping to help Miss London on the secondhand book stall. She asked me to bring some old books to sell.

Oh, that's good! I was tidying the study, when I found some of your old annuals and spy novels. You can take those.

5

Aren't you going to dress up, Anna? You normally love the costume competition.

Yes! And Mr. McMaster has invited the mayor of Aceton to give the prizes to the winners.

Oh, no! The costume competition is for little kids! I don't want to dress up this year.

6 On Saturday ...

Come on! Miss London told us to arrive early.

Don't forget, Anna. You must hold Bongo's lead. He mustn't run around the fair.

7 At the fair, Anna was selling books …

… when Bongo saw a squirrel.

8 First Bongo chased the squirrel around the maypole.

9 Then Bongo ran through the skateboarders …

10 Next Bongo ran through the secondhand clothes stall.

11 And after that, Bongo ran past the smoothie stall.

12 Finally the squirrel climbed up a tree and Bongo stopped.

Vocabulary and Reading

1 **Match the words with the pictures (1–12). Listen, check and say.** 🎧 80

> cozy   crowded   dangerous   deserted   freezing   historic
> mountainous   noisy   rural   snowy   tropical   urban

2 **Look at Text A. Listen and say the adjective.** 🎧 81

Last year's vacation

A **My Arctic Adventure**

Me at Heathrow Airport, London

View from the plane

Goodbye, England!

At Polar Bear Lodge

Me in the Arctic!

B

Nobody here!

Polar bear!

How to survive in the Arctic

Make a snow shelter

- You can't dig a snow shelter on flat snow, so first look for a slope.
- Check you have about 2 meters of snow for your shelter.
- With a shovel, dig an entrance tunnel, which should be about 1 meter long.
- Then start digging out the snow. The roof and the walls of the shelter should be at least 60 centimeters wide.
- If there are trees nearby, put branches on the floor so that you are not touching the snow.
- Put a backpack in the entrance to keep out the wind.
- If possible, light a candle to give you light and warmth.

3 **Read Text B and answer.** ⏱ 1 min

- What do you need to make a snow shelter?

4 **Ask and answer in pairs.** 💬

> What sort of places do you like?   I like urban places, especially big noisy cities.

5 Read and listen. Which word best describes Uncle Greg's trip?

C

Day 1

Dear Alex,

I'm writing my diary, because I promised to write it for you every day. I've just arrived in Canada and I'm going to travel to the Arctic tomorrow. Hurrah! I've been to tropical jungles and mountainous deserts, but I've never been to the Arctic!

Your very excited Uncle Greg

Day 2

I'm here! At the moment I'm at Polar Bear Lodge. We flew here by helicopter over the Churchill River and I saw seals and a wolf. There are nine people on the tour and our guide's name is Felix. I hope you are working hard at school!

Day 3

Something terrible has happened! Today we went on an expedition in the snow buggy. We were going to the Arctic sea when Felix asked me, "Have you ever seen an Arctic hare?" "No, I haven't," I said. He told us he could see some hares, so we got out of the buggy to watch them. One hare ran behind some trees and I followed it, because I wanted to take a photo. But when I came back, the group and Felix weren't there! Now I'm sitting on my backpack in the snow all alone. Have you ever been lost? It's a horrible feeling! I'm going to wait here for Felix and the group. I hope they come soon!

P.S. I didn't even get a photograph of that hare!

Still Day 3

Oh, dear! Where are Felix and the group?! It's very cold! I've never been this cold before! I'm in my tent now, but it's very windy. In fact it's very, very, very windy …

Still Day 3, but nearly Day 4

Sorry about that! My tent blew away! Have you ever dug a snow shelter? I have! I'm in it now! (I'm glad I read that Arctic survival guide before I came here!) I've put some branches on the floor and I've lit a candle. Outside it's -50 degrees, but it's very cozy in here! What an adventure!

Day 4

I woke up very early and lit a fire outside my snow shelter. I was making a cup of tea when I heard a noise. It was Felix in the snow buggy! He saw the smoke from my fire and came to rescue me! (He couldn't return yesterday because the snow buggy broke down and then the storm began.) Now I'm back at Polar Bear Lodge and I'm safe. Phew! More adventures tomorrow …

 6 Answer in pairs. Use the phrases in the box.

1 On which day did Uncle Greg arrive in the Arctic?

2 Why did he go behind the trees on Day 3?

3 What happened when he was behind the trees?

4 Where did he sleep? Why?

5 How did Felix find him?

6 Where was Uncle Greg on Day 4?

Because he / she / it /they …

I (don't) think they …

On which day did Uncle Greg arrive in the Arctic?

He arrived on …

1 Look at page 89. Read and listen to the story again. Match the sentence halves.

1 Have you ever seen an Arctic hare?

2 Have you ever been lost?

3 I have never been

4 Have you ever dug a snow shelter?

a I have! I'm in it now.

b No, I haven't.

c It's a horrible feeling.

d this cold before.

2 Complete the chart.

Present Perfect (*have* + past participle)						
Questions				**Affirmative**		
Have	you / they	ever	gotten lost?	I / They	**(1)** ____have____	flown in a helicopter.
Has	he / she		slept in a tent?	He / She	**(2)** _____	seen an Arctic hare.
Short answers				**Negative**		
Yes,	I	have.	No,	I	haven't.	I / They	**(3)** _____	flown in a helicopter.
	he	has.		he	hasn't.	He / She	**(4)** _____	seen an Arctic hare.

3 Listen and number.

4 Ask and answer in pairs.

visit a historic place

sunbathe on a tropical beach

fly over a mountainous region

see a dangerous animal

be lost in a crowded place

sleep in a cozy tent

Have you ever been lost in a crowded place?

No, I haven't.

1 **Read part 1 and complete. Read Text B on page 88 again and check.**

1

How to survive in the Arctic
Make a snow shelter

- You can't dig a snow shelter on **(1)** _____flat_____ snow, so first look for a slope.
- Check you have about **(2)** _____ meters of snow for your shelter.
- With a shovel, dig an entrance tunnel, which should be about **(3)** _____ meter long.
- Then start digging out the snow. The roof and the walls of the shelter should be at least **(4)** _____ centimeters wide.
- If there are trees nearby, put branches on the floor so that you are not touching the **(5)** _____.
- Put a **(6)** _____ in the entrance to keep out the wind.
- If possible, light a candle to give you **(7)** _____ and warmth.

2

Drink water

- It's important to drink lots of water in the Arctic. If you don't have any water, don't worry!
- You can light a camping cooker inside your snow shelter. Make a small hole in the roof above the stove so the gas can escape out of the shelter.
- If you don't have a cooker, make a fire outside. You can then melt some snow in a pan.
- If you don't have a pan, you can put some snow into a clean item of clothing, for example, a sock. Tie the item of clothing to a stick so that it hangs over the fire. Put a cup below, so the water can drip into it.

2 **Read part 2 and match the pictures with the words.**

| **a** above | **b** below | **c** outside | **d** inside | **e** into | **f** over |

1 _a_   2 ___   3 ___   4 ___   5 ___ 6 ___

3 **Read, look and complete.**

Boot Room Rules

- Leave your skis **(1)** _____outside_____.
- Bring your other equipment **(2)** _____.
- Put all your wet clothes **(3)** _____ the drier.
- Put your hats and gloves into the box **(4)** _____ your name.
- Put your goggles onto the shelf **(5)** _____ your name.

1 **Look and say what the lesson is about.**

2 **Listen and repeat.** 🎧84

look forward to

get on

get off

set off

get on with

run out of

fall out with

look after

put up

make up

put out

do up

3 **Listen and number the verbs.** 🎧85

- [ ] get on with
- [1] make up
- [ ] set off
- [ ] look forward to
- [ ] run out of
- [ ] do up

4 **Complete the sentences with the correct verbs from Activity 2.**

1 I always stand in a line before I can _____<u>get on</u>_____ the bus to school.

2 I want to make a cake, but I've _____ sugar. So I'll try it with honey.

3 I often _____ my little sister when my mom is busy.

4 I sometimes _____ my best friend. Then we don't talk to each other.

5 I _____ my aunt. We have a lot of fun together.

6 It's important to _____ a fire after you finish cooking.

5 Listen to the song. Mark (✔) the verbs you hear. 🎵🎵 86

- ☐ fall out with
- ☐ look after
- ☐ put up
- ☐ get on
- ☐ look forward to
- ☐ run out of
- ✔ get off
- ☐ make up
- ☐ set off
- ☐ get on
- ☐ put out
- ☐ do up

6 Listen again and complete the song.

The bus arrives and we **(1)** ____get off____.
We're in the forest. Let's **(2)** _____!
Exploring, in the forest.
We've got a lot to learn about.
There's not much water. Don't run out!
Exploring, in the forest.

Exploring, in the forest.
We're learning, in the forest.
Life's cool, in the forest.
Exploring, in the forest.

(3) _____ a shelter made of wood.
Now it's finished. It looks good!
Exploring, in the forest.
We get on well and we don't fight.
We all **(4)** _____ the night.
Exploring, in the forest.

Exploring, in the forest.
We're learning, in the forest.
Life's cool, in the forest.
Exploring, in the forest.

We **(5)** _____ stories 'round the fire,
(6) _____ the fire when we're tired.
Exploring, in the forest.
Do up your sleeping bag. Keep warm.
We're lucky there's no thunderstorm!
Exploring, in the forest.

Exploring, in the forest.
We're learning, in the forest.
Life's cool, in the forest.
Exploring, in the forest.

7 Read and circle the correct answers.

1 The explorers travel to the forest by …
   a bus.   **b** car.

2 They … a lot of water.
   a have   **b** don't have

3 They put up …
   a a shelter.   **b** a tent.

4 The explorers … each other well.
   a fall out   **b** get along with

5 They tell stories … the tent.
   a inside   **b** outside

6 There … a storm.
   a is   **b** isn't

8 Look at the pictures in Activity 2 and tell the story in pairs. 💬

Miss London is looking forward to camp.

The day arrives and she gets on the bus.

1 Look at the pictures and say what you think about space vacations in the future.

2 Listen, read and check your ideas.

Fewer than six hundred people have ever been into space, but in the future, more people will be able to travel there. A space vacation will begin with three days of medical checks and training in a spaceport. The travelers will learn about safety and they will practice some techniques used by NASA astronauts.

The day before the space flight, the travelers will get on a special plane, but they won't go into space. They will watch a spaceship take off.

On the day of the flight, the travelers will put on special suits and get on the spaceship. There will be five passengers and two pilots. They will fly to 50,000 feet (15,240 meters). Then they will listen to the countdown to the speed of sound! After 90 seconds, the pilots will turn off the engine, but the spaceship won't stop. It will continue to climb to 360,000 feet (110 kilometers above the Earth).

The passengers will leave their seats. They will be able to float in zero gravity and enjoy views of Earth from large windows for about 4–5 minutes and there will be total silence. They will then return to Earth to their friends and family, who will be waiting in the spaceport lounge.

About 350 people have already booked to go to space, but a seat on a spaceship will cost about US $200,000 dollars, so it won't be a cheap vacation.

3 Look at the chart and underline more examples of *will* and *won't* in the text.

Will			Won't		
The travelers	will	learn about safety.	It	won't	be a cheap vacation.
The spaceship		travel at the speed of sound.	They		live in space.

4 Read the text again and write *true* or *false*.

1 Space travelers will practice techniques used by pilots.   _false_

2 The day before the space flight they will get on a special plane.   _____

3 The travelers will wear ordinary clothes on the space flight.   _____

4 Each space flight will have five passengers.   _____

5 The passengers will have to stay in their seats.   _____

6 The space vacation won't be expensive.   _____

5 Correct the false sentences in pairs.

Space travelers won't practice techniques used by pilots.

They will practice techniques used by astronauts.

1 Look at the vacation pictures in pairs. Which one do you want to go on? Why?

2 Listen to the dialogue and underline. 🎧 88

1 Mr. Bean is going to book a vacation …

  a on the phone.

  b in a travel agency.

  c on a website.

2 Alex wants to go to the beach because he …

  a likes snorkeling best.

  b likes swimming best.

  c likes diving best.

3 Anna wants to go to the countryside because she …

  a prefers sleeping in a tent to a hotel.

  b prefers cycling to diving.

  c doesn't like cities.

4 Lily wants to go camping because she …

  a doesn't like beaches.

  b prefers walking to cycling.

  c likes sleeping in a tent best.

3 Complete the sentences from the dialogue. Then listen again and check.

1 Alex: Can we go to the beach? I like diving ___best___ .

2 Anna: Let's go to the countryside! I _____ cycling to diving.

3 Lily: Can we go camping, please? I _____ sleeping in a tent best.

4 Anna: That's awesome! I prefer snow _____ sunshine!

4 Look, listen and repeat. 🎧 89

Perfect Pronunciation

I'm going to book a vacation.   Let's go to the countryside!   We're going to go skiing.

Can we go to the beach?   I prefer cycling to diving.   I prefer snow to sunshine.

5 Complete the pairwork cards. Ask and answer in pairs. W B 125

Where do you want to go? Do you like the mountains or the beach best?

I like the mountains best.

Latitude

1 **Listen and read along. Match the questions with the pictures.** 🎧 90

1 **What is the Equator?**

When you look at a globe, there is a line around the middle of the Earth. It is an imaginary line drawn on maps. It is called the Equator, and it is halfway between the North Pole and the South Pole. The Arctic is at the North Pole. It is the most northern point on the Earth. The South Pole is the most southern point on the Earth.

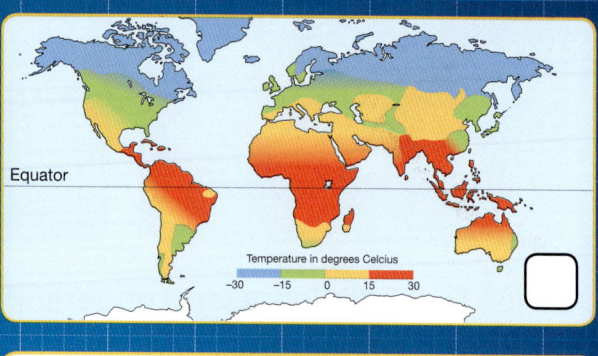

2 **What is latitude?**

Latitude lines on maps measure the distance between a place on Earth and the Equator. The Equator is 0 degrees. The latitude of the North Pole is 90 degrees north. The latitude of the South Pole is 90 degrees south.

3 **Why is latitude important?**

Latitude tells us how hot or cold a place is. The temperature in places near the Equator is higher than in places further away from the Equator. For example, Tanzania's latitude is 6 degrees south. It is very hot. Iceland's latitude is 65 degrees north. It is very cold. The Poles are furthest away from the Equator and they are also the coldest places on Earth.

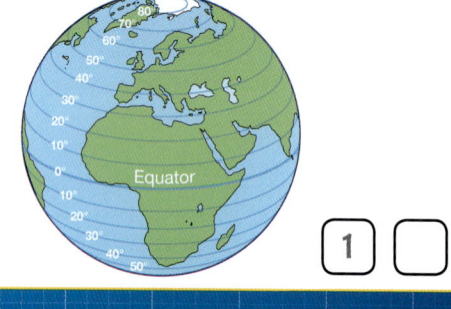

1

4 **Why are the Poles cold?**

The sun is directly over the Equator. That means that places close to the Equator get strong sunlight. The Poles are cold because the sun is at an angle, so the heat is spread over a bigger area. Near the Equator, the light and the heat are strong. Further away from the Equator, there is less light and heat.

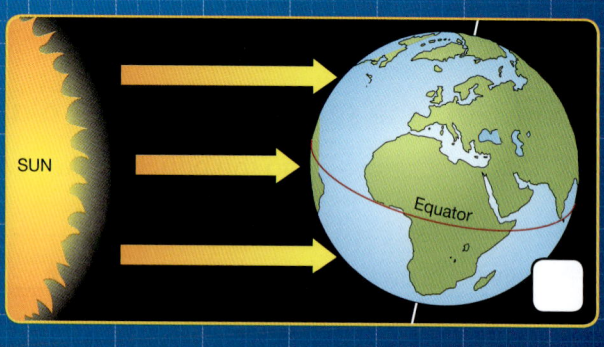

2 **Read again and complete the mind map.** 📝

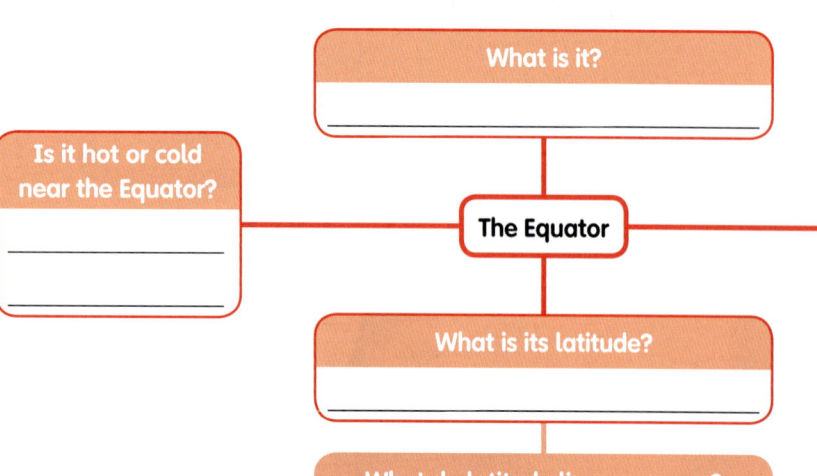

What is it?

_____

What is the latitude of the South and the North Pole?

_____, _____

Is it hot or cold near the Equator?

_____

The Equator

Where is it?

Halfway between the

North and the South Pole

What is its latitude?

_____

Where are the South and North Pole?

_____

What do latitude lines measure?

_____

1 **Read Alex's composition. What's Alex's opinion of vacations in the future?**

a They will be similar to vacations now.   **b** They will be better than vacations now.

- <u>Introduction</u>
  Write some general information about the topic.

- <u>Main ideas</u>
  Use topic sentences and give examples in your writing.

- Use "I think that" and "I believe that" to give your opinions.

- <u>Conclusion</u>
  Use "To sum up" in your conclusion and finish your writing with a strong opinion.

Vacation of the Future by Alex Bean

Today we often go on summer vacation to the beach. Or we go to the countryside or historic towns and cities. But, in the future, I think that there will be different kinds of vacation.

I think that people will vacation in space. For example, people will visit the Moon and there will be Moon station hotels with lots of air, water and food so travelers won't run out of these things. Travelers will be able to float inside big domes with no gravity. It will be very relaxing!

Another vacation of the future will be underwater vacations. I believe that there will be submarine hotels in tropical oceans. The hotels will have glass walls so people can see the colorful fish in the water. Travelers will also be able to walk on the seabed in glass tunnels with lots of ~~lites~~ lights.

To sum up, vacations in the future will be great. People won't want to go to noisy, crowded places when they can visit quiet and relaxing places above the Earth or under the sea.

Punctuation

We use a capital letter for the first letter of days and months, but not seasons.

August

summer

2 **Read the composition again and answer the questions.**

1 How does Alex describe vacation today?

2 How many types of vacation of the future does he describe?

3 Describe the differences between them.

4 Which vacation would you prefer?

5 Do you agree with Alex's conclusion?

6 Which mistake did Alex make in his text? Why?

3 **Write a composition about summer vacations in the future.**

Phonics
Silent letters

1 **Listen and read. Circle the silent letters.** 🎧 91

In summer on Wednesdays, Silent D
Invites all the silent letters for tea.
Silent B combs his hair and climbs on a chair.
Silent H asks questions, "When, why and where?"
Silent W answers, but his answers are wrong.
Silent T often listens to Christmas songs.
Silent K knocks, then comes in on his knees.
He's got a knife and he knows there is cheese.
Today is the day silent letters meet,
So ssh! Be quiet! (And wipe your feet!)

2 **Read again and write the words with silent letters.**

World Temperature Thermometer

Alex's Value ...

Materials

* Poster paper
* Rolls of different colored cardboard
* Colored pens

★ **Read and stick.**

Be careful in the sun. Don't get sunburn!

Stage 1: Plan your project.

1. Work in pairs. Look at a map of the world. Find the equator. Find different cities, some that are near the equator and some that are far from the equator.

2. Research the climate of the different cities. What do you notice? What is the climate like in the cities closest to the equator?

 ### Stage 2: Develop your project.

1. With your partner, make a thermometer out of rolls of cardboard. Cover the cardboard in different colors representing the climates from very hot (red) to very cold (purple). Put the thermometer onto poster paper.

2. Write the names of the cities next to the correct color on the thermometer. Put the hottest cities next to the red and the coldest cities next to the purple. Draw country flags next to each city.

Stage 3: Share your project.

1. Show your thermometer to other groups.

2. Talk about the temperature of different places. Explain the relationship between the location of a city on the globe and the distance of that place from the Equator.

Stage 4: Evaluate your project.

Save your *World Temperature Thermometer*.

Temperatures Around the World

Caracas		Kuwait
Bangkok		Dar el Salaam
Darwin		Cairo
Chennai		Rio de Janeiro
Mexico City		Tokyo
Istanbul		Buenos Aires
Canberra		Madrid
Paris		New York
Berlin		Astana
Warsaw		Kathmandu
Ottawa		Oslo
Bucharest		Moscow

red = extremely hot
orange = hot
yellow = quite hot

light blue = mild
dark blue = cold
purple = extremely cold

1 **Look and write questions.**

1 Have you ever been kayaking? _____
2 _____
3 _____
4 _____
5 _____
6 _____

2 **Look and complete the sentences.**

1 The school of the future will be on the Moon _____ .

2 Students _____ .

3 Everyone at school _____ .

4 The school uniform _____ .

5 P.E. class _____ .

3 **Read and complete the text. Use the correct phrasal verb.**

School Camp Report

We **(1)** ___got on___ the bus outside the school gates and we arrived in Acebury at 9 o'clock. Then we **(2)** _____ the bus, put on our backpacks and **(3)** _____ for the woods. We found a good place to camp and we **(4)** _____ our tents. In the afternoon Lily **(5)** _____ Alex, because he put a beetle in her boot! In the evening we **(6)** _____ ghost stories around the camp fire. We **(7)** _____ the fire before we went to bed. In the night I had to **(8)** _____ Lily because she was scared of the dark! Poor Lily!

Cool Cooking
homework
_____

Find out about
food from another
country.

Vocabulary and Reading

1 **Match the words with the pictures (1–12). Listen, check and say.**  92

bean sprouts brown sugar chilies cucumber garlic lime
noodles oil peanuts pepper shrimp spring onions

2 **Look at Text A. Listen and say the food.** 93

3 **Read Text B and answer.**  1 min

- Which item on the shopping website isn't in the recipe?

A

Showing products 1-8

2	1 Liter	$1.45	Quantity − 1 + ADD
3	Pack 50 g	$0.50	Quantity − 1 + ADD
4	Bunch	$0.65	Quantity − 1 + ADD
5	Each — BUY ONE GET ONE FREE	$0.30	Quantity − 1 + ADD
6	Whole each	$0.80	Quantity − 1 + ADD
7	Each	$0.85	Quantity − 1 + ADD
8	500 g — HALF PRICE was $1.40 now $0.70	$0.70	Quantity − 1 + ADD

B

Pad Thai noodles

Ingredients

- 175 g rice noodles
- 3 ½ tablespoons sunflower oil
- 12 large raw shrimp
- 2 garlic cloves

- ½ red chilli
- 2 medium eggs
- 3 tablespoons Thai fish sauce
- Juice of 1 lime
- 6 spring onions

- 1 tablespoon brown sugar
- 4 tablespoons roasted peanuts
- 50 g bean sprouts

4 **Ask and answer in pairs.**

How often do you eat the food on this page?

I often eat cucumber.

5 Read and listen. Which text is fact and which is fiction?

1 4,000 years ago there was a town called Lajia in North West China.

> This is a good harvest! There's a lot of millet this year.

> Yes! We have enough food for all the people of Lajia.

2 The people of Lajia made flour with the millet. Then they made noodles from the flour.

> Yum! Delicious noodles, Jun! Thank you!

> You eat too many noodles, Li! You're getting fat!

3 Suddenly the earth began to move. It was a terrible earthquake.

> Quick, Li! Run! There isn't enough time to finish your noodles.

4 Then the Yellow River burst its banks.

> There's too much water! Let's climb on the roof!

The World's Oldest Noodles
Report by J. J. Journalist
Aceton Daily News, October 14, 2005

A team of archeologists have found a bowl of 50 cm-long yellow noodles under the ground in North West China. They believe the noodles are about 4,000 years old.

The team also found skeletons of people in this area. "We believe there was a big earthquake and the people were trying to run away," Professor Wang told reporters. "One of these people was probably eating noodles when the disaster happened."

Professor Wang, aged 42 from Shanghai, China, believes these noodles are made from millet flour and not wheat flour like modern noodles.

"The discovery is very exciting for the people of China," he said. "Before we found these 4,000-year-old noodles, nobody knew which country invented noodles. Now we know the truth. Noodles are Chinese!"

6 Answer in pairs. Use the phrases in the box.

1 Did Li finish his noodles? Why?

2 What did the archeologists find in 2005?

3 How are noodles today different to the old noodles?

4 Why was the discovery important?

> Because he / she / it / they …
>
> I (don't) think they …
>
> They're different because …

> Did Li finish his noodles? Why?

> No, he didn't, because …

1 Look at page 101. Read and listen to the story again. Match the sentence halves.

1 Why weren't the people of Lajia hungry?

2 Why wasn't Li thin?

3 Why did Jun and Li climb on the roof?

4 Why didn't Li finish his noodles?

a Because there wasn't enough time.

b Because there was too much water.

c Because they had enough food.

d Because he ate too many noodles.

2 Complete the chart.

Quantities (*too much* / *too many* / *enough*)						
Countable nouns				**Noncountable nouns**		
Affirmative	She has	**(1)** _____	chilies.	She has	**(4)** _____	rice.
	He has	**(2)** _____	peanuts.	He has	**(5)** _too much_	water.
Negative	He doesn't have	**(3)** _enough_	shrimp.	He doesn't have	**(6)** _____	time.

3 Listen and number.

 1

4 Look at the recipe and the people's ingredients. Play the game in pairs.

Max
20 shrimp
200 g rice
200 g peanuts
3 chilies
20 g oil
1 pepper

Recipe for Thai Stir Fry
300 g rice
20 shrimp
150 g peanuts
3 chilies
20 g oil
2 peppers

Leo
12 shrimp
300 g rice
100 g peanuts
1 chili
40 g oil
2 peppers

He doesn't have enough shrimp.

It's Leo.

1 Read part 1 and complete. Read Text B on page 100 again and check.

1

Pad Thai noodles

Ingredients
- 175 g (1) _rice noodles_
- 3 ½ tablespoons sunflower oil
- 12 large raw
  (2) _____
- 2 garlic cloves
- ½ red (3) _____
- 2 medium
  (4) _____
- 3 tablespoons Thai fish sauce
- Juice of 1
  (5) _____
- 6 spring onions
- 1 tablespoon brown sugar
- 4 tablespoons roasted
  (6) _____
- 50 g bean sprouts

2

Method

1 Before you begin, peel the shrimp, chop the chili and slice the spring onions. Beat the eggs and squeeze the lime.

2 Boil the noodles in salted water. Drain and mix with ½ tablespoon oil.

3 Heat the rest of the oil in a frying pan. Add the peeled shrimp and stir-fry for 1½ minutes. Then add the garlic and chopped chili. Cook for ½ minute more.

4 Pour in the beaten eggs and stir-fry them for 10 seconds. Then add the cooked noodles, fish sauce, squeezed lime juice and brown sugar. Toss everything together for 1 minute until the noodles are hot.

5 Add the roasted peanuts, sliced spring onions and bean sprouts. Toss together for 1 minute and serve.

2 Read part 2 and order the pictures (1–6).

3 Find the phrases in part 2 and match.

roast → _roasted_

1 peel → _____
2 squeeze → _____
3 slice → _____
4 chop → _____
5 cook → _____
6 beat → _____

4 Look and write instructions.

1 **Look and say what the lesson is about.** 💬

2 **Listen and repeat.** 🎧 96

	Country	Nationality
1	France	French
2	Poland	Polish
3	China	Chinese
4	Spain	Spanish
5	Italy	Italian
6	India	Indian

3 **Listen and complete the sentences.** 🎧 97

1 This cheese is _____French_____ .

2 This pizza is _____.

3 This curry is _____.

4 This special fried rice is _____.

5 These dumplings are _____.

6 This potato omelet is _____.

4 **Write sentences with the dishes, countries and nationalities from Activity 2.**

cheese   curry   dumplings   fried rice   pizza   potato omelet

1   This cheese is from France. It's French.

2   _____

3   _____

4   _____

5   _____

6   _____

5 Listen and mark (✔) the nationalities you hear. 98

- ✔ American
- ☐ Indian
- ☐ Mexican
- ☐ Chinese
- ☐ Italian
- ☐ Polish
- ☐ French
- ☐ Jamaican
- ☐ Spanish

6 Listen again and number the verses in order.

A ☐

Chinese rice
Is always nice.
And so is Indian curry
We have French cheese
Jamaican peas,
But an Italian take-out is faster.
Hey! An Italian take-out is faster.

B ☐

Have you tried
A hot Pad Thai?
Or delicious Polish dumplings?
And don't forget
Spanish omelet!
Or we can eat Italian pizza
Hey! Or we can eat Italian pizza.

C 1

In the US, there is every kind
of dish
We can eat anything that we wish
We can eat tacos
And we can eat French fries
Or we can eat Italian pizza!
Hey! We can eat Italian pizza.

7 Listen again. Circle the correct answer.

1 The country in the song … Japan.
   a is   (b) isn't

2 The singer … Chinese food.
   a likes   b doesn't like

3 … is in the song.
   a A pizza   b Pasta

4 The cheese in the song is from …
   a Spain.   b France.

5 The peas in the song are from …
   a Jamaica.   b India.

6 The singer's favorite food is …
   a curry.   b pizza

8 Ask and answer in pairs.

Which food is spicy?

Indian curry is spicy.

Which food …

- has rice?
- has a lot of garlic?
- is spicy?
- is typical in the US?
- is made from flour?
- is made from potatoes?

1 Look at the photos. Say what you know about how to make spaghetti.

2 Listen, read and check your ideas.  99

Spaghetti is a very popular food and is eaten all over the world, but have you ever wondered how it's made?

Spaghetti is made of flour and water. Traditionally, it's made of a special kind of wheat called durum wheat, which is grown in Italy. The wheat is made into flour and the flour is mixed with warm water in the spaghetti factory. Sometimes different colors or flavors are added to the spaghetti.

After that, the mixture is stretched and rolled into thin sheets. Then it's pushed through small holes to create long thin pieces. (The name *spaghetti* means *thin string*). It's cut into pieces of about 25–30 centimeters. Longer lengths of 50 centimeters used to be popular.

Next, the spaghetti is hung up and dried.

Finally, the spaghetti is packaged. The packets are transported all over the world to shops and supermarkets.

Spaghetti isn't eaten raw. We have to cook it. It's boiled in water and it's served with many different sauces and cheese. Which one is your favorite?

3 Look at the chart and underline more examples of the simple present passive in the text.

Simple Present Passive					
Durum wheat	is	grown in Italy.	The packets	aren't	transported to shops.
Spaghetti	isn't	eaten raw.	Colors	aren't	always added.

4 Read the text again and write *true* or *false*.

1 Durum wheat is grown in Jamaica. _false_

2 Pasta is made from flour. _____

3 Flavors are always added to pasta. _____

4 The flour is pushed through holes. _____

5 Factory workers dry spaghetti. _____

6 The packets of spaghetti are left in the factory. _____

7 We eat cooked spaghetti. _____

5 Correct the false sentences in pairs.

Durum wheat isn't grown in Jamaica.

It's grown in Italy.

1 Look at the pictures and answer in pairs. Which meal is your favorite?

2 Listen and complete the information. Circle the correct meal in Activity 1. 🎧 100

Drink: _____

Appetizer: _carrot soup___

Entree: _____

Side dish: _____

3 Listen again and underline Mrs. Bean's answers.

1   Are you ready to order?
   a   Yes, I am.
   b   Can I have another minute, please?

2   What would you like for the entree?
   a   Can I have carrot soup, please?
   b   I'd like carrot soup, please.

3   What would you like for the main course?
   a   I'd like spaghetti with tomato sauce, please.
   b   I'll have spaghetti with tomato sauce.

4   Anything else?
   a   Yes, a green salad, please.
   b   Can I have a green salad, please?

5   What would you like to drink?
   a   A glass of orange juice, please.
   b   Can I have a glass of orange juice, please?

4 Look, listen and repeat. 🎧 101

Perfect Pronunciation

Are you ready to order?   I'd like carrot soup, please.   A glass of orange juice, please.

Anything else?   Can I have a green salad, please?   Yes, of course.

5 Complete the pairwork cards. Ask and answer in pairs. WB 126

Are you ready to order?

Yes, I am.

Alex Knows about ...

Energy Balance

1 Listen and read along. Look at the food label and write the numbers. 🎧 102

34g carbohydrates   ___ fat   ___ protein

Your body needs energy from protein, carbohydrates and fat in food and drinks to work well and to stay healthy. Your body uses energy all the time: when you are walking, running, eating, thinking or sleeping. If you are very active, your body uses more energy. The amount of energy you get from food is energy input. The amount of energy your body uses is energy output.
We measure energy input in calories. The number of calories in food or drinks is how much energy we get when we eat or drink. In one gram of protein there are four calories. In one gram of carbohydrate there are four calories. In one gram of fat there are nine calories. If food is in a package, you can usually see the number of calories on the label.
Calories give us the energy we need to do everything in our day. Our Basal Metabolic Rate (BMR) is the amount of calories our body uses to keep us breathing and keep our heart beating. A person's height, weight, gender and age changes their BMR. If you are very active, you need a lot more calories than your BMR. If you aren't very active, you don't need many more calories than your BMR.
It is important to have an energy balance. That means the energy input and output have to be balanced. If you are not very active, you do not use the energy from your food. Then the body stores the energy from your food as fat in your body. But if your energy input is not high enough for your BMR, this is dangerous because your body can't work properly.

Nutrition Facts
Serving Size: 1 cookie (50g)
Servings Per Container: 22

Amount Per Serving	
Calories 220	Calories from Fat 80 Calories

	% Daily Value*
Total Fat 9g	14%
Saturated Fat 5g	25%
Trans Fat 0g	
Cholesterol 35mg	12%
Sodium 160mg	7%
Total Carbohydrate 34g	11%
Dietary Fiber 3g	8%
Sugars 20g	
Protein 4g	

Vitamin A 6%	•	Vitamin C 0%
Calcium 2%	•	Iron 4%

*Percent Daily Values are based on a 2,000 calorie diet. Your daily values may be higher or lower depending on your calorie needs:

	Calories:	2,000	2,500
Total Fat	Less than	65g	80g
Sat Fat	Less than	20g	25g
Cholesterol	Less than	300mg	250mg
Sodium	Less than	2,400mg	2,500mg
Total Carbohydrate		300g	375g
Dietary Fiber		25g	30g

2 Read again, look at the chart and follow the instructions.

Energy Input and Energy Output for Sam–11 years old

Energy Input		Energy Output	
Food and Drinks	**Calories**	**Activities**	**Calories**
breakfast	450	walking to school	60
snacks	230	walking back home	60
drinks	270	playing football for 1 hour	280
lunch	650	doing chores in the house	110
dinner	720	BMR	1555
Total		Total	

1 Complete the total for Energy Input and Energy Output.

2 Are the Energy Input and Energy Output balanced?

3 Look at the chart and think of three ways to balance the Energy Input and Energy Output.

1 Read the letter. What kind of letter is it?

a a letter of invitation   **b** a thank-you letter   **c** a letter of apology

- Write the address at the top.

- Write the date under the address.

- Start the letter with "Dear" and the name of the person.

- Say why you are writing the letter, and give some interesting information.

- Finish the letter with "From" and your name.

Bean Cottage
Little Street
Aceford
Acefordtown
AC1 23E

Tuesday, March 14

Dear Mr. Semolina,

I'm writing to say thank you for the tour of the spaghetti factory. It was fantastic! Now we know that durum wheat is grown in Italy and spaghetti is made from ~~flower~~ flour. It was very interesting and your workers are very skillful.

I'd also like to thank you for the free packets of spaghetti at the end of the tour. Everybody in our class loves Italian food, so we were very happy. I made spaghetti with a chili, shrimp and tomato sauce for dinner when I got home.

Thank you again!

From

Lily Bean and Class 5A
The Ace School

Punctuation

Use a comma after Dear and the name of the person you are writing to.

Dear Mr Semolina,

2 Read the text again and answer the questions.

1 Who is the letter to?
2 When did Lily write the letter?
3 Where does Lily live?
4 What did Lily learn at the factory?
5 What did Mr. Semolina give Lily?
6 Which mistake did Lily make in her letter? Why?

3 Write a thank-you letter to a friend.

Phonics
Homophones
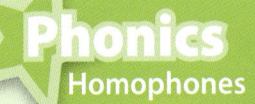

1 Listen and read. Circle the foods. 🎧 103

Here are the chefs. They know what to do.
They meet at the (meat) shop at two.
They've picked pairs of pears. They've read a red book.
They've been to the bean shop. They're ready to cook.
The maid has made cakes. Don't they look great?
(Before there were ten, but the chefs ate eight.)
She has flour on her hands and a flower in her hair
Whether the weather is cloudy or fair.

2 Read again and write the pairs of homophones.

Energy Balance Plan

Materials

* Ruler and pencil
* One sheet of poster board
* Colored pens and pencils

★ Read and stick.

Be active and eat healthy amounts of food to have energy balance.

Stage 1: Plan your project.

1. Divide the sheet of poster board into two parts. Use your ruler and pencil to draw an *Energy Output and Input* chart on the left.

2. Decide if the plan is for a boy or a girl.

Stage 2: Develop your project.

1. Write on the chart the amount of food the boy or girl will eat and the activities he / she will do in one day. Calculate the calories used and the Basal Metabolic Rate like this:

   Boys (17.5 × weight in kg) + 651

   Girls (12.2 × weight in kg) + 746

3. Draw the boy or girl doing a light or heavy activity on the right part of the poster board.

Stage 3: Share your project.

1. Attach your *Energy Balance Plan* on a classroom wall. Walk around and look at the other plans.

2. In small groups, discuss: Is the energy input and output of the boy or girl balanced? If not, what needs to happen to achieve an energy balance? Why?

Stage 4: Evaluate your project.  98

Save your *Energy Balance Plan*.

Energy Balance Plan

Energy Output

Intensity	Activity Type	Minutes	Hours of Activity (minutes ÷ 60)	Calories Used (hours × calories)
VERY LIGHT 85 cal/hour	Watch T.V	150	150÷60 = 2.5	2.5×85 = 212
LIGHT 140 cal/hour	walk to school	30	30÷60 = 0.5	0.5×140 = 70
MODERATE 285 cal/hour	riding a bike	20	20÷60 = 0.33	0.33×285 = 95
HEAVY 400 cal/hour	Swimming class	60	60÷60 = 1	1×400 = 400
Total Energy Output (BMI:1,451+ Energy Output of Activities)				2,228

Energy Input

Food or Drink	Food Label (serving size)	Number of servings in my portion	Food Label (calories per serving)	Total Calories (number of servings × calories per serving)
Breakfast	scrambled eggs	2	385	2×385 = 770
Lunch	cheese sandwich and fruit	1.5	575	1.5×575 = 862
Snack	potato chips	8	196	8×196 = 1568
Dinner	stews and soups	1	685	1×685 = 685
Total Energy Input				3,885

Billy doesn't have energy balance. He needs to exercise more. He can spend less time watching TV and more time in his swimming class. He can eat healthy snacks, like fruit, instead of chips.

1 **Read and write the missing words.**

5A Bake Sale By Alex Bean, 5A

Mr. Fit was worried because we didn't have **(1)** _____enough_____ sports equipment for P.E. Class 5A wanted to help.

We **(2)** _____ cakes and cookies and **(3)** _____ them on Saturday morning. At 9:30 am there were no more cakes and cookies because **(4)** _____ people wanted to buy them. We had to make some more!

We raised **$128.00!** Now we have **(5)** _____ soccer balls and tennis balls for P.E.

2 **Look and write sentences.**

plan newsletter

write text

draw pictures

check newsletter

copy newsletter

give copies to students

1   The newsletter is planned.

2   _____

3   _____

4   _____

5   _____

6   _____

3 **Look and write the words.**

The winner of the school raffle is …
Miss London!

1st **PRIZE** Food hamper

1 oil_____

2 c_____

3 s_____
   o_____

4 w_____

5 b_____
   s_____

6 p_____

7 n_____

8 l_____

4 **Find and write the countries.**

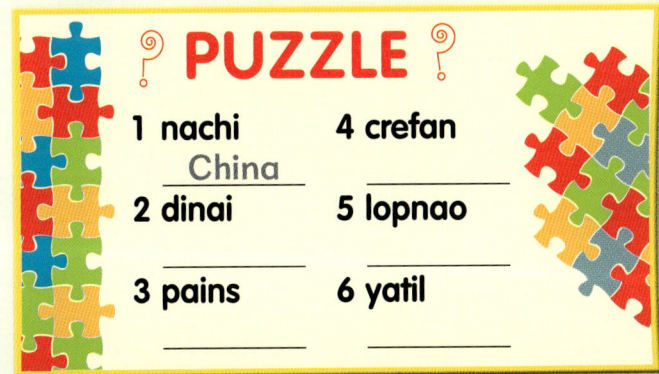

⸮ PUZZLE ⸮

1 nachi
__China__

4 crefan
_____

2 dinai
_____

5 lopnao
_____

3 pains
_____

6 yatil
_____

Dazzling Drama homework

Find out about setting up a play.

1 Play *Six in a Row.*

Italy

1 **Match the words with the pictures.**

[ ] chocolate [1] pasta [ ] pizza

2 **Read and match the headings with the paragraphs.**

[ ] Celebrating special food [ ] Sweet things in Italy [1] Popular food

Italy is in Europe. The capital city is Rome. People in Italy speak Italian. Tourists come from all over the world to see the architecture in Italy's historic cities and its famous museums and art galleries, but perhaps Italy is most famous for its wonderful food.

1 Pasta is very popular in Italy. There are over 500 different kinds of pasta, including ravioli, spaghetti and linguine. But the most famous food from Italy is pizza. The first pizza restaurant opened in Naples in 1830. The most popular kind of pizza is a pizza margherita. It is made with tomatoes, mozzarella cheese and basil leaves. They are red, white and green, and these are the colors of the Italian flag. Families often go out together to a pizza restaurant on the weekend.

2 Every part of Italy has different dishes. People in Italy like going to food festivals. Food festivals are called *sagre*. They celebrate a food, for example: fish, garlic, cheese, mushrooms or nuts. Hundreds of dishes are made with the food. Everyone sits at long tables and shares the food. There's also music and fun!

3 Italians like sweet food, too. They eat cookies, pastries or cakes for breakfast. They dip them in coffee or warm milk. And Italians also like chocolate. There are many chocolate festivals in Italy. People drink chocolate, eat chocolate and cook with chocolate. There are even sculptures made out of chocolate.

 3 **Read again and complete the Venn diagram with foods.**

Italy   Where I Live

Both
chocolate

113

9 Dazzling Drama

1 Match the words with the pictures (1–12). Listen, check and say. 🎧 104

> audience   backstage   cast   costumes   curtain   director
> lighting designer   lines   props   scenery   sound technician   stage

2 Look at Text A. Listen and say the words. 🎧 105

A

THE PRINCE'S PRIZE

BY Suzanne Torres

It's a play within a play

B

Fun for the Whole Family!

The Prince's Prize, the new play by Suzanne Torres, brings together some of your favorite fairy tale characters!

You'll see some of the cast from *Goldilocks*, *Sleeping Beauty*, *Snow White*, *Cinderella* and more!

The play is set in a theater, where all the cast are practicing for a play. They hear that the prince, who is the owner of the theater, is coming to give one of them a prize!

Who is the prize for?

All your favorite characters

3 Read Text B and answer. ⏱ 1 min

- What is the play about?

4 Play a guessing game in pairs. 💬

> Actors wear these.   Costumes!

5 Read and listen. Who has won the prince's prize?  106

Scene 1: On stage at the theater

[THE ACTORS ARE ON STAGE. ENTER THE DIRECTOR, HOLDING A CELL PHONE.]

DIRECTOR: [EXCITEDLY] Stop everyone! The prince is coming! He's the owner of this theater and he has a special prize for one of us.

SEVEN DWARFS: [ONE WORD EACH] Who … is … the … prize … for, … Mr. … Director?

DIRECTOR: I don't know, but I can guess! I'm an excellent director and I get fantastic reviews in the newspaper …

BIG BAD WOLF: The prize isn't for you! It's for me! I'm famous all over the world!

SLEEPING BEAUTY: You're famous for wearing Grandma's nightgown, Wolf! And children are scared of you! Children love me! The prize is mine!

UGLY SISTER 1: [ANGRILY] Don't be silly, Sleeping Beauty! You're the laziest actor in this theater!

UGLY SISTER 2: You're only interested in sleeping! We dance all night at the palace.

ELVES: And who makes your dancing shoes, Sisters? We do! We work all night. We're good at making costumes.

QUEEN: Oh, I'm tired of listening to you all. [LOOKING IN HER MIRROR] The prize is mine, because I'm the most beautiful in the land.

MIRROR: Sorry, but you're not the most beautiful. Goldilocks is more beautiful.

BABY BEAR: Goldilocks! I'm very angry with her! She ate my porridge again! And I'm sad about my broken chair. [STARTS TO CRY]

DIRECTOR: [QUICKLY] Wait! Can you hear that? [SOUND OF ROYAL TRUMPETS] It's the prince!

Scene 2: Backstage at the theater

PRINCE: I was very excited about coming to the theater.

CINDERELLA: [COMING INTO THE ROOM WITH A BROOM] Oh, I'm sorry!

DIRECTOR: Shh, Cinderella!

PRINCE: The prize is for a very special person who is always friendly to people. This person helps the cast when they're worried about going on stage or bored with learning their lines. This person listens to the director when he's sad about getting a bad review. And the theater is always nice and clean because of this person. Yes, this special prize is for … the one and only … Cinderella!

CINDERELLA: Oh, thank you! Wow! It's a magic lamp!

6 Answer in pairs. Use the phrases in the box. 💬

1 Why does the director think the prize is for him?

2 Why shouldn't the wolf get the prize?

3 Why shouldn't Sleeping Beauty get the prize?

4 Do you agree with the prince's choice?

Because he / she …

He / She should / shouldn't get the prize because …

I (don't) think he / she should get the prize because …

Why does the director think the prize is for him?

Because he gets fantastic reviews.

1 Look at page 115. Listen to the play again and choose the words. 106

  1 The wolf is (famous for) / scared of / excited about wearing a nightgown.

  2 Baby Bear is **friendly to** / **angry with** / **worried about** Goldilocks.

  3 The prince is **worried about** / **excited about** / **tired of** coming to the theater.

  4 Cinderella is **friendly to** / **worried about** / **angry with** people.

2 Complete the chart.

Adjectives and Prepositions			
to be	excited / worried / sad / happy / angry	(3) _____	something / doing something.
	angry / good / bad	at / with	
	tired / scared	(4) _____	
	(1) _____ famous _____	for	
	(2) _____	in	

3 Listen and number. Complete the sentences. 107

  1 The prince is __friendly to__ Cinderella.

  2 The Ugly Sister is _____ dancing.

  3 The elf is _____ sewing.

  4 Goldilocks is _____ Daddy Bear.

  5 Mommy Bear is _____ making porridge.

  6 The queen is _____ the mirror.

4 Describe and guess the pictures in pairs.

He's sad about his leg.

Number 5!

1 Complete the advertisement leaflet. Read text B on page 114 again and check.

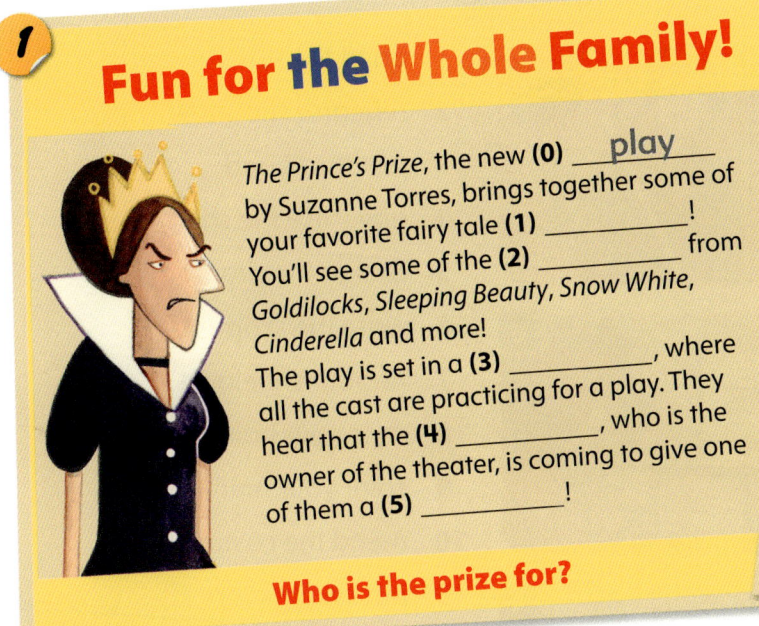

1

Fun for the Whole Family!

The Prince's Prize, the new **(0)** __play__ by Suzanne Torres, brings together some of your favorite fairy tale **(1)** _____! You'll see some of the **(2)** _____ from Goldilocks, Sleeping Beauty, Snow White, Cinderella and more!
The play is set in a **(3)** _____, where all the cast are practicing for a play. They hear that the **(4)** _____, who is the owner of the theater, is coming to give one of them a **(5)** _____!

Who is the prize for?

2

Is the prize for the Elves, who work *hard* making costumes for the cast?

Is it for the Director, who directs very *well*?

Is it for the Wicked Queen, who dresses *beautifully* but isn't very kind?

Is it for Sleeping Beauty, who learns her lines very *slowly* and snores *loudly*?

Is it for the Ugly Sisters, who talk *angrily* to Cinderella, but love the Prince?

Or is it for Cinderella, who cleans up *cheerfully* all day and has to run *fast* at midnight?

The cast wait *hopefully* … but does it all end *happily*? To find out, you'll have to come and see the show!

Tickets available now! Call Box office (989) 098-4847.

2 Read part 2 and answer the questions in pairs.

3 Read again and complete the chart. What do these adverbs describe?

Adjective	Adverb	Adjective -y	Adverb	Adjective -ful	Adverb	Adjective	Irregular Adverb
clever	cleverly	happy	**(1)** happily	beautiful	beautifully	good	well
loud	loudly	angry	angrily	hopeful	**(3)** _____	hard	hard
slow	**(2)** _____					fast	**(4)** _____

4 Use the pictures to write a story. Include adverbs from Activity 3.

1 Look and say what the lesson is about. 💬

2 Listen and repeat. 🎧 108

1 build the set
2 rehearse the show
3 test the sound
4 advertise the show
5 design the programs
6 write the script
7 tie your shoelaces
8 style your hair
9 color your hair
10 mend the costumes
11 put on makeup
12 paint your nails

3 Listen and order the phrases. 🎧 109

| 1 | building the set | | styling hair | | testing the sound |

| | designing the programs | | rehearsing the show | | writing the script |

4 Complete the Venn diagram with the actions from Activity 2. Which actions could go in both circles? 📝 💬

Jobs the actors do

rehearse the show

Both

Jobs the Theater staff do

5 Listen and mark (✔) how the singers are feeling. 🎵 110

bored and grumpy ☐   excited and happy ☐   tired, but happy ☐

Alex's Tune

6 Listen again and complete the lyrics.

> Who advertises our big show?   Who mends the costumes when they tear?
> Who has to paint their nails   Who rehearses everything that they know?   ~~Who designs the program~~

Who writes the script and writes the songs?
I do!
Who learns their lines the whole night long?
I do!
(1) _Who designs the program_
In time for the show?
The program design is something I know.
Who puts up posters, do you know?
I do!
(2) _____
I do!
Who builds the set and tests the sound, too?
I do!
And I do!
We do it for the show!

(3) _____
I do!
Who has to curl and style their hair?
I do!
(4) _____
And put makeup on?
I have to do it and I think it's fun.
Who dyes their hair purple and green?
I do!
Who ties shoelaces between scenes?
I do!
(5) _____
We do!
And we do!
We do it for the show!

7 Mark (✗) the lines that are not in the song.

1 ☒ Who tests the sound?

2 ☐ Who advertises our big show?

3 ☐ Who mends the costumes when they tear?

4 ☐ Who dyes their hair orange and yellow?

5 ☐ Who ties shoelaces between scenes?

6 ☐ Who rehearses everything that they know?

8 Play *Memory* in groups. 💬

I work in a theater and I write the script and I test the sound …

I work in a theater and I write the script …

I work in a theater and I write the script and I test the sound and I put on makeup …

1 Look at the photos and say what you know about *The Lion King*.

2 Listen, read and check your ideas. 111

The Lion King

The Lion King is a famous stage musical. It's an adaptation of the animated movie by Disney, with music by Elton John and song lyrics by Tim Rice. It opened at the Lyceum Theater in London's West End on October 19, 1999 and it's still running.

The Lion King tells the story of a lion called Simba. When Simba is a little cub, his father, Mufasa, dies. Simba thinks he killed his father, so he runs away. When he's older, his cousin Nala finds him and he returns to his homeland to become king.

The characters in the musical are all animals. There are 25 species of mammals, birds, fish and insects.

The costume designer has special animal costumes made for the actors. She has lots of enormous puppets and African masks built, too.

To prepare for each performance of the show, 114 people are needed. The actors have their hair styled and their huge masks put on before the show. The actress who plays Rafiki has her hair braided and her face painted red, yellow and blue. Some of the other actors have their bodies painted. It's a very colorful and spectacular show!

There have been more than 28,000 performances of *The Lion King* musical all over the world, and more than 50 million people have seen it.

3 Look at the chart and underline more examples of *have something done* in the text.

Have Something Done (*have* + object + past participle)			
The costume designer	has	special animal costumes	made.

4 Read the text again and write *true* or *false*. Correct the false sentences.

1 The costume designer makes the animal costumes. ___false___

2 Somebody makes the puppets and masks for the costume designer. _____

3 Somebody puts the masks on the actors. _____

4 The actress who plays Rafiki braids her hair. _____

5 Somebody paints Rafiki's face. _____

5 Say true sentences about the actors in pairs.

> learn their lines   cut their hair   sing the songs   mend their costumes
> write the script   rehearse the play   take their photos   paint their faces

> The actors learn their lines.

> They have their hair cut.

1 **Look at the movie listings and write the movie ratings.**

1 PG

2

3

NEW RELEASES

★ ★ ★ ★ ★ Movie World ★ ★ ★ ★ ★ 01234 01234

Date	Movie	Rating	Price
September 22	Castle of Cobwebs	G	$7.50
September 30	Jungle Volcano II	PG	$7.50
	Pirate Island	PG	
October 1–31	Three Babies and a Man	PG-13	$6.50

2 **Listen to the dialogue and write the name of the movie that is chosen.** 🎧 112

Movie: _____

3 **Listen again and number the sentences in the order you hear them.**

a ☐ I don't like cartoons very much.

b 1 Why don't we watch a horror movie?

c ☐ Good idea! It's a PG, so we can watch that.

d ☐ Romantic movies are boring!

e ☐ Let's watch a comedy.

f ☐ How about that movie with the ship on the cover?

4 **Look, listen and repeat.** 🎧 113

Perfect Pronunciation

scary	boring	funny	pretty	island
cover	actor	pirate	babies	castle

5 **Complete the pairwork cards. Ask and answer in pairs.** 📖 127 💬

Let's watch a romantic movie!

How about a spy movie?

I don't like romantic movies very much.

1 Listen and read along. Write down an example of each of the elements in a play that you have seen or read. 🎧 114 📝

Lily Knows about ...

Changing a Story into a Play

| costumes | dialogue | props | scene location | sound effects | stage directions |

Stories in books are often made into plays or musicals, which we can see in the theater. But books and plays are very different. When you read a story, you make pictures of the characters and scenes in your mind. But when you watch a play, you see a story in the same way that the director and the scriptwriter see it. When you change a book into a play, there are many things to think about.

1 In a book, there is description. This tells us what is happening. In a play, there are stage directions. Stage directions tell the actors where they should be on the stage and what they should be doing or saying.

2 In a book there is a description of the characters. We can read about what they are thinking and how they are feeling. But in a play we learn about the characters through the dialogue. The dialogue is what they say. We also learn about the characters by how they speak and the expressions on their faces. The costumes and props give even more information about the characters.

3 In a book there are chapters. In a play, there are scenes. Scenes can move the action forward in time by five minutes, five days or five years. A new scene can also change the location. It is always written at the beginning of the scene where and when the scene is set.

4 In a book, there is a description of background sounds, like a storm. In a play these become sound effects giving information about what is happening. Sound effects can also change our feelings. Music can make us feel scared or happy. Slow footsteps or a loud crash can make us feel frightened.

2 Read again and change the sentences from the book into a playscript. 📝

1 Cinderella sat by the fire. She could hear her sister's carriage go down the street. She felt so sad. She really wanted to go to the ball. "I will never go to a ball," she cried.

2 Suddenly there was a bright light. A fairy godmother appeared. She smiled kindly at Cinderella and said, "You will go to the ball." Cinderella still looked sad. "I can't go to the ball," she said. "My clothes are all gray and old."

1 Read the playscript. What kind of play is it?

a a play with a happy ending   **b** a play with a funny ending   **c** a play that isn't finished

- Write where the characters are and what they are doing.
- Write who is speaking.
- Write stage directions in parenthesis.
- Write adverbs in parenthesis to tell actors how to say the line.

Grandma's Attic by Lily Bean

Scene 1

[WILLIAM AND BETTY ARE AT WILLIAM'S GRANDMA'S HOUSE. THEY ARE GOING UP THE STAIRS TO THE ATTIC.]

BETTY: [NERVOUSLY] We've never been up these stairs before.

WILLIAM: [HAPPILY] I know! I'm excited about seeing Grandma's attic! Where's the key? Let's open the door!

[BETTY OPENS THE ATTIC DOOR WITH THE KEY.]

BETTY: [QUIETLY] Oh! It's very dark!

[WILLIAM FINDS THE LIGHT SWITCH.]

WILLIAM: [IMPATIENTLY] The light doesn't work.

BETTY: [SLOWLY] I'm scared of the dark, William.

WILLIAM: Don't worry! I have a flashlight!

BETTY: [NERVOUSLY] Turn it on quickly!

[WILLIAM TURNS ON THE FLASHLIGHT AND SHINES IT AROUND THE ATTIC.]

BETTY: Oh! Look at all these spider webs!

WILLIAM: [WORRIEDLY] And look at all these boxes!

BETTY: What's in them?

WILLIAM: Instruments. My grandma's a <u>musision</u>. We have to move them so Grandma can have the roof fixed.

[SUDDENLY THE CHILDREN HEAR A STRANGE NOISE.]

BETTY: [NERVOUSLY] What was that noise?

WILLIAM: [EXCITEDLY] I don't know. It came from behind that curtain!

Punctuation

Use exclamation marks (**!**) to show strong feelings like surprise, anger, fear or humor.

Don't worry**!**

2 Read the text again and answer the questions.

1 Who are the characters?
2 Where are they and why?
3 What is it like there?
4 Who is nervous and why?
5 What do you think the noise is?
6 Which mistake did Lily make in her text? Why?

3 Write the ending of the play in Activity 1.

Phonics
Spellings of words ending with /ʃn/

1 Listen and read. Underline the jobs. 🎧 115

Today there's a Talent Show sensation!
Here are directions and an invitation.
First on the stage is the <u>magician</u>.
He's famous for magic. He's on television.
He waves his wand and puts on his black cloak.
There's an explosion, with lots of green smoke.
Now it's dark. It's not an illusion.
The lights have gone out and there is confusion.

All the audience makes conversation.
The electrician arrives from the station.
Then on the stage it's the musician,
'Til the writer of fiction stands in position.
The politician has some suggestions,
And if you like, you can ask her questions.
The Talent Show is for you and me.
With inventions, collections and lots to see.

2 Read again and write the words with the /ʃn/ sound.

Fun Play Script

Anna's Value ...

Materials

* ★ Paper and pens
* ★ Props
* ★ Costumes

★ **Read and stick.**

Be respectful during a performance!

Stage 1: Plan your project.

1 Work in groups. Think about stories you know well. Choose a short story that you want to make into a play.

2 Decide who is going to play which character. Plan the props, sound effects and costumes you need. Think about how all the characters are going to say their dialogue.

Stage 2: Develop your project.

1 Work together to write a play script. Include stage directions.

2 Create your props and costumes.

3 Practice your performance.

Stage 3: Share your project.

1 Perform your play for the rest of the class.

2 Look at the audience: is everyone interested in your play?

Stage 4: Evaluate your project.  110

Save your *Project Record*.

1   Read the definitions and complete the *Glossary*.

audience   (n) the people who watch a show

_____ (n) the part of the stage the audience cannot see

_____ (n) the actors in a show

_____ (n) clothes for actors

_____ (n) it opens on the stage before a show

_____ (n) the person who gives actors instructions

_____ (n) a kind of designer at the theater

_____ (n) the actors have to learn these

_____ (n) the objects used on stage during the play

_____ (n) big pictures at the back of a stage

_____ (n) the person who operates the sound during a play

_____ (n) where the actors stand

2   Use the words to write sentences.

angry   clever   excited   friendly   ~~interested~~   scared

1   I'm interested in acting.

2   _____

3   _____

4   _____

5   _____

6   _____

3   Look and write sentences.

Have a great summer break!

1 Mr. McMaster has his car washed.

School Trip

1 **Listen and read the story.** 🎧 116

1

Let's get on the train now, everyone!

I've never been to France. I'm excited about this school trip!

So am I! It will be fantastic.

2

You're all good at finding out information, so here's a quiz about Paris. Please give me your answers at the end of the trip.

3

Paris Quiz

(1) It's 50.45 km long.   T_ _ C_ _ _ _ _ _ T_ _ _ _ _

(2) You can see these in the sky on July 14.   F_ _ _ _ _ _ _ _

(3) It's 15 cm shorter in the winter than in the summer.   T_ _ E_ _ _ _ _ T_ _ _ _

(4) It's a traditional dish.   F_ _ _ _ O_ _ _ _ S_ _

(5) You can see a pyramid here.   T_ _ L_ _ _ _ _ M_ _ _ _ _

(6) He was a famous French writer.   E_ _ _ _ _ R_ _ _ _ _ _

4

We're in the Channel Tunnel now! The sea is above us!

Yes, we're about here. The journey through the tunnel takes about 35 minutes. It's 31.35 miles, or 50.45 kilometers long.

That's the answer to the first question!

5 The next day in Paris.

It's very crowded and noisy here!

There's a quiz question about that, but I can't see anything in the sky.

That's because it's July 14. It's Bastille Day, which is a special day in France.

I can see The Eiffel Tower over there! Let's have our photo taken at the top!

6 At the top of the Eiffel Tower.

Phew! There are too many steps!

I'm scared of heights!

The Eiffel Tower is painted every 7 years. It's 324 meters tall, but it's …

… 15 centimeters shorter in the winter!

It's the answer to Question 3!

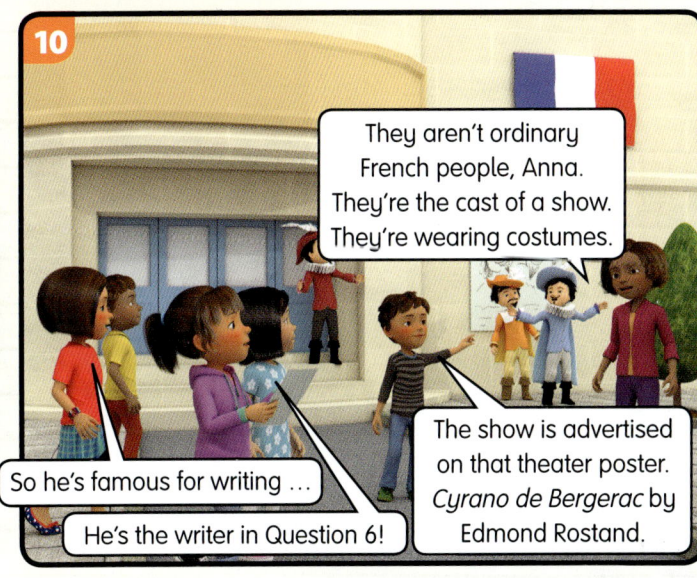

127

Syllabus	Vocabulary	Structures	Pronunciation and Phonics	Cross-Curricular Themes	Cultural Values
S	Places in a School Physical Descriptions	What…? When…? *How many…? Do you…?*			
1	Bugs In the Garden	Simple Present Present Continuous Zero Conditional	Stress in compound nouns Spellings of the sound /əʊ/	Science: Honeybees	Protecting the environment
2	TV Programs Money	Comparative and superlative adjectives with two or more syllables Infinitives of purpose / adjectives with infinitives with *to*	Saying dates and numbers Spellings of the sound /aɪ/	Math: Using Graphs	Respecting Others
3	Materials Ancient Rome	*be made of* Simple Present and Past *Used to / didn't use to*	Intonation in lists Spellings of plurals	Literature: The Rosetta Stone	Being responsible and careful
4	Adjectives to Describe People Types of Books	Past Continuous / Simple Past Simple Past with *wh-* questions	Saying letters Long vowel with Magic E	Literature: Parts of a Story	Taking care of books
5	Adventure Sports Equipment and Clothing	Verb patterns with infinitives (verb + infinitive with *to* / verb + object + infinitive with *to*) Modal verbs of obligation	Sentence stress and weak forms Spellings of the sound /eɪ/	Science: The Respiratory System	Exercising to keep healthy
6	Everyday Objects Adjectives to Describe Objects	Present Perfect 1 Relative Pronouns	Word stress in longer adjectives Spellings of the sound /uː/	Art: Sculpture	Being kind and showing respect
7	Adjectives to Describe Places Phrasal Verbs	Present Perfect 2 *Will / won't* (future fact)	Sentence stress and weak forms (schwa /ə/) Silent letters	Geography: Latitude	Being careful in the sun
8	Food Countries and Nationalities	Describing quantity (*too much, not enough*) Simple Present Passive	Intonation in sentences Homophones	Science: Energy Balance	Being active and healthy
9	Theater Words Behind the Scenes Phrases	Adjectives and prepositions *have* + object + past participle	Word Stress Spellings of words with /ʃn/ endings	Drama: Changing a Story into a Play	Being respectful during a performance

Value Stickers

Achievement Stickers